Herta F. ...pa-Tuskany

...ies

A Complete ... wner's Manual
Translated by ... nd Robert Kimber

With Color Photographs by Well-Known Animal
Photographers and Drawings by Günther Marks

D0791109

BARRON'S

Front cover: The change from bridle to halter or vice-versa should be done slowly and deliberately. The reins hang over the right arm in this process.
Inside front cover: Two Island ponies playing together.
Inside back cover: A test in cross-country riding. The cross-country rider and his pony have to be able to cope with every kind of terrain.
Back cover: above left, riding a Shetland bareback; above right, Shetland pony mare with her foal; below left, Falabella pony with upper lip drawn back; below right, Haflinger pony with pony wagon.

First English-language edition published 1984 by Barron's Educational Series, Inc.
Second edition 1986

© 1983 by Gräfe and Unzer GmbH, Munich, West Germany

The title of the German edition is *Ponys.*

All inquiries should be addressed to:
Barron's Educational Series, Inc.
250 Wireless Boulevard
Hauppauge, New York 11788

International Standard Book No. 0-8120-2856-2

PRINTED IN CHINA

56   490   9876

Book Credits
Hans Scherz, series editor
Renate Weinberger, volume editor
Heinz Kraxenberger, cover designer

Photo Credits
Alder: page 46,
Angermayer/Hellabrun Zoo: page 26 (center right),
Animal/Wilbie: page 17 (center left),
Animal: page 17 (center right),
Dossenbach: page 17 (above left, below left and right);
page 28 (above right, below left and right); page 45 (above);
page 55; inside back cover; back cover (above right),
Francke: inside front cover; page 18 (above),
Hawkes: page 28 (center left); back cover (above right),
Münker: page 56 (above),
Ramm: page 17 (above right),
Reinhard: page 28 (above left),
Skogstad: front cover
Zimmerman: page 18 (below); page 45 (below); page 56 (below); back cover (above left).

Note and Warning
In this manual pony fanciers and owners will find information on the purchase and care of a pony, also advice on riding and driving. Because a pony is a powerful and often temperamental animal, every pony rider and owner has to take it upon himself to recognize the dangers and to take steps to avoid them. Parents of young riders are urged to instruct their children with this in mind.

You will find "Rules for Handling a Pony" on page 65. The sections "A Basic Riding Course" on page 67 and "Learning to Ride" on page 68 contain detailed information on the necessity for riding instruction.

Adequate insurance is in your own interest. Liability insurance for the pony owner should be regarded as a necessity. But it is also recommended for riders and the parents of children who ride. Also recommended—as for any sport—is accident insurance.

Children and beginners who are still inexperienced with ponies should handle a pony only with supervision and after appropriate instruction.

Rides on a pony or cross-country trips with a pony wagon or sleigh should always be made in groups or with several participants, and they should always be led by experienced riders or drivers.

It is advisable, before setting out on a ride or drive, to tell a responsible person where you will be going and how long you expect to be out.

Contents

Ponies

Ponies are small horses with big personalities. They have highly developed characters, intelligence, and temperament, but they are often not taken quite seriously. Their small size and undemanding natures lead people to assume that there are no particular requirements for their care and grooming. I acquired my first pony when I was living in Argentina. I had horses at the time, and I thought I could give my pony the same kind of care I gave the horses. My expectations soon proved incorrect. Only through long contact with my pony did I learn what was required to keep it in a way appropriate to its nature. A book about ponies would have been a great help to me, but I was unable to get one in the Argentine back country where I was. As a result, I learned through experience what a pony's needs are. Over the years, I have accumulated valuable experience, which I pass on to anyone who likes ponies, is keeping them now, or wants to keep them.

In this book I give advice that will enable you to keep your pony as a pony should be kept, to feed and care for it properly and conscientiously. This information will be of interest not only to pony owners but also to those who borrow or rent ponies, for they are often required to take over care and feeding. How to keep your pony healthy is a crucial issue, and this handbook provides you with measures you can take to prevent illness, describes signs of illness, and explains possible treatments. I am grateful to Dr. Horst Linhart of Grafing, West Germany, a veterinarian and breeder of Shetland ponies, and to Dr. H. A. Müller of Roth in the Lahn Valley, a veterinarian and breeder of Haflinger ponies, for reading and checking the chapter on health.

I have always been fascinated by the variety of pony breeds. On my travels through many countries of Europe, Africa, and the Americas I have visited stud farms to learn more about the origins, development, and characteristics of various pony breeds. This information is crucial for choosing a pony, for understanding its nature, and for giving it proper care. For this reason, I have provided detailed descriptions of the most popular pony breeds, accompanying the descriptions with color photographs. The text calls attention to the versatility of ponies as well as to their background and the work to which they are best suited. From these descriptions, the reader will see that ponies are not—as I once read somewhere—a "compromise between what we might want and what we can get" but that they can meet all our demands for leisure and sport. There are available today ponies suitable for children, young people, and adults, for beginners and competitive riders alike.

I offer some hints and suggestions on the vast subject of riding and driving, but do not expect extensive instruction on these activities. There are specialized books on them, and some of these books are listed on page 69. It is amazing what a healthy, robust pony is capable of and what a great variety of things we can do with our small companions in our free time.

What Is a Pony?

Everyone knows that a small horse is called a pony. But no such clarity exists about how the pony acquired its name and what exactly makes a pony a pony. This is not too surprising since there are major differences among the various breeds, which range from tiny miniature ponies to elegant small horses. The contrast between these two extremes is just as great as that between a heavy (draft) horse and a graceful Arabian.

One important characteristic of many breeds is the close resemblance of these ponies to their ancestors, the wild horses of the Paleolithic age. Ponies that have the stocky build, heavy coat, and full mane and tail typical of primitive horses come closest to the general notion of what constitutes a pony. But since, apart from these almost primeval-looking ponies, there are other and different basic types, people often ask if there is any one characteristic that is common to all ponies.

The most obvious trait shared by all ponies is their nature, the typical pony disposition. It combines charm, liveliness, and a degree of individuality that can border on willfullness with high performance, hardiness, and modesty of needs.

Do ponies, then, really differ from horses? I once spent some time on a large riding farm. The stables were occupied almost exclusively by full-size horses. The riding activities—in the indoor and outdoor rings and on the jumping course—took place almost in silence. The large yard and the stables that surrounded it were quiet except for the occasional snorting of a horse. This riding farm held regular courses for riding and jumping ponies, and riders from far away would attend with ponies of all breeds. As soon as they arrived, the yard and stables were filled with bustling life. I would be awakened early in the morning by long, ringing whinnies, the calls and answers of the small, sturdy pony stallions. Then the entire riding area was filled with the excited clopping of small hoofs, motion, and high spirits, even during hard training. When the course came to an end and the ponies were loaded into their trailers and driven off, quiet would return. But whenever I heard cheerful whinnying in the yard and pasture I knew that those lively and eager pint-size creatures, the ponies, were back.

When Is a Small Horse a Pony?

In a book written around the turn of the century I found the following definition of a pony: "A horse of very small stature, often standing no more than 8.2 to 10 hands (85 to 100 cm) high and never more than 14 hands (140 cm), therefore dwarf-like." The size or, more accurately, the small size is regarded as the distinguishing feature of the pony. This is generally still true today, although the internationally accepted standard lies above "dwarf-like." The height at the withers is what counts,

This is how a pony scratches behind the ear.

What Is a Pony?

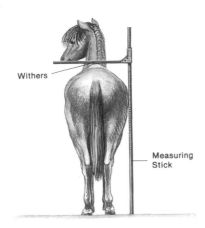

Withers

Measuring Stick

This is how you measure a pony: The measuring stick touches the side of the pony, and the cross piece rests on the highest point of the withers.

and 14.2 hands (147.3 cm) is the cutoff point. A pony cannot measure more than 14.2 hands. This is important for breeding purposes as well as for entering competitions and shows. But apart from this arbitrary, external characteristic there are other features that distinguish ponies from horses—features that have to do with their general nature and that make them so endearing to us.

The Origin of the Word *Pony*

The word *pony* was first used in Great Britain, where these animals have long played an important role and where there are several native pony breeds. The word probably derives from the French *poulenet,* an old form of *poulain,* which means "foal." *Poulain* goes back to *pullanus* in medieval Latin, and *pullus* was the original Latin term for a young animal and for a foal.

Before You Buy

Your Own Pony—Dreams and Reality

What horseback rider does not have the ardent wish to own a horse? He or she would like to cultivate a bond with the animal not only while showing or riding cross-country but also in the daily routine of feeding and care and in taking personal responsibility for the animal's well-being. In the case of a large horse, this involves great expense, which usually stands in the way of realizing the dream. The same is not true for a pony. Until a few years ago, ponies were kept almost exclusively as pets for children, to be ridden only by children and to pull buggies for them. Ponies were hardly ever considered as mounts for larger riders. But now that the pony has grown more and more popular for recreational use, young people and adults have the opportunity of realizing their dream of owning their own mount.

A pony usually costs much less to buy than a full-size horse, and the upkeep is usually much less, too. Housing a pony is also less involved. Of course, we must not forget that the duties and responsibilities toward the creature "horse" are basically the same, whether we are talking about a large or a small one. And we should also keep in mind that ponies generally live longer than large horses and that their character or temperament can sometimes be a trial for the owner.

The notion that a pony can be kept "somehow, somewhere, on the side" is wrong. In practice it almost always has detrimental effects for the pony and leads to disappointment and discouragement on the part of the pony's keeper. You can avoid such negative experiences if you give serious consideration to what is actually involved in keeping a pony before you purchase one. This is particularly important if the pony is intended for children. Even a short ride on a rented pony can spark ecstasy in a child and inspire dreams of having such a small four-legged companion, of petting its warm, shaggy coat every day. Children picture themselves riding their "horsey" around home as easily and safely as they did the rented pony, and they have no idea that keeping a pony means not only having fun but also taking on work and responsibility. They have no way of knowing how much space and feed a pony needs or how much patience and consistent work its care and training demand.

Children who belong to a pony club or have spent vacations on a pony farm usually have a more realistic view and are aware of what it takes to keep a pony. In their case it is unlikely that initial excitement will give way to disenchantment and loss of interest.

How deep a child's desire is for a pony of his or her own becomes evident in the persistence with which the desire is reiterated to the parents. If the child also makes sacrifices to realize the dream—saving his allowance, for instance, or offering to do chores at home, or working in the stable of a nearby riding club —it is time for the parents to think of getting a pony and to consider seriously all the aspects of such a move. It is best if the questions that come up are discussed by the whole family together and as realistically as possible. A child will hardly be able to take care of his or her pony without occasional help from parents and siblings. If everything is left up to the child there is no guarantee that the pony will get adequate care. But—and this should be settled from the very beginning—the young owner, the child himself, should feel that the pony is his responsibility.

Requirements for Keeping a Pony

The necessity of providing adequate living conditions for a pony brings up some basic questions:
• Where should I house my pony? In a barn

of my own close to the house, in an open shelter with paddock and pasture, or board him at a stable or riding club?
• Do the pony's quarters meet its special needs?
• Can my pony graze on a pasture at least part of the time?
• Do I have enough time for my pony? For grooming, feeding, and exercising it regularly, for cleaning out the stall or maintaining the pasture and keeping the fence in good repair? Am I really willing to devote several hours a day to my equine companion?
• Can I provide my pony with adequate exercise not only in good weather but also in bad?
• Will my pony be properly looked after when I am away or am prevented for one reason or another from doing it myself? Who will take over my duties at those times?
• Do I have the financial resources not only to buy and equip a pony but also to meet the running expenses for housing, feed, for the veterinarian, the blacksmith, and for the absolutely essential insurance (see page 14)?

I raise these questions not to discourage you or dampen your enthusiasm but simply to call your attention to some practical considerations that arise if you are going to have a pony. Once these questions are properly solved, prospects are good that the future pony owner will be able to truly enjoy his new companion.

The Qualities You Want in a Pony— How You Will Use It

Those of you who want a pony will have a clear idea about what you want it for. You should also know what qualities and character traits are necessary for the intended use so that you will then be able to select your pony for those qualities. Since the range of pony breeds is very wide, the choice is not easy. I would therefore advise you to consider carefully beforehand which pony is best for you. In the descriptions of the common breeds (page 14) the suitability of different ponies for various uses is mentioned.

The pony's exterior—its appearance and size—should match its new tasks as much as its character or temperament—its interior makeup—does. But the inner qualities take precedence. This is especially true of ponies that are going to be around children. Such a pony has to be reliable; that is, it has to be good-natured and easy to handle. It should not bite, kick, rear, shy, or become unmanageable under any circumstances. Young, untrained ponies are therefore out of the question. An older, well-trained pony is ideal for a child, particularly if it is his first riding animal. Since a pony that receives good care can be ridden or driven for a long time—usually over twenty years—buying an older pony makes good sense. Many basically docile ponies can also be quite lively. These are not appropriate for timid or fearful children, but intrepid and energetic young riders can deal with them easily, gain confidence, and learn a lot about riding. When you choose a pony for a child you therefore have to think not only about the characteristics of the pony but also about the nature of the child.

One more thing to mention in this context is that four to six years is usually considered the minimum age at which children should be exposed to ponies. It is impossible to state an absolute rule because individual children vary so much. My daughter was no more than two years old when she used to sit on the back of my horse when it was resting in the shade of a eucalyptus tree (we were living in South America at the time). When she was four years old and after repeated requests, she received her first pony. In the case of very small children, the size of the pony is crucial. Children should trust their ponies from the very beginning. This trust is gained most quickly if the "horsey" is not a giant but a manageable companion. Ponies to be considered for this age group are the traditional breeds for children such as the Welsh Mountain, the Shetland, and small crossbreeds. The Shetland pony is the most popular. It gets along well with children and makes an excellent playmate since it can be ridden and used for driving. It takes to the harness readily and is strong enough to pull several children—and even adults—in a cart. Keep in mind that children grow quickly, their legs get longer, and they will soon refuse to ride a little pony because their feet "drag on the ground."

Most ponies are suitable for driving. This is of particular interest if you live in the country. Riding in a horse-drawn buggy or, during wintertime, a sled is getting increasingly popular.

Ponies kept in suburban areas at a boarding stable are used primarily for pleasure riding and for show jumping and eventing. Larger ponies of aristocratic appearance are preferred here. They should have good equestrian qualities, a lively temperament, and long, smooth gaits. Connemara, Welsh Cob, Haflinger, and the Pony of the Americas are some of the breeds that come to mind here. Good schooling is, or course, also desirable. Most of the larger pony breeds are suitable for family use such as cross-country riding and for weekend and long-distance rides. They can be kept outside if they are healthy and robust.

A Foal or a Grown Pony?

No child can resist a pony foal, and the charm of these amusing, shaggy little creatures works its magic on adults as well. The desire to raise and train a pony foal is therefore easy to understand. But raising a pony and training it later requires knowledge and experience as well as a great deal of time and patience. It takes years before the pony is ready to be ridden or harnessed to a cart. In addition, dealing with a spirited young pony is difficult and not without danger—at least for children and beginners.

Foals do best if they are allowed to play, tussle, and chase after each other. Ponies should grow up in the company of others their age, not alone.

Ponies grow up slowly. Some breeds require more time to reach full maturity than most full-size horses. The Icelandic pony, for instance, cannot be ridden until it is at least five years old. If it has to carry loads prematurely, injuries and weaknesses of the spine and legs can occur and may show up years later. This is true of all ponies. Anyone who is looking for a pony should therefore think twice before choosing a foal, no matter how irresistible it may be. Grown ponies—preferably older and well-trained ones for children and beginners—are a better choice because they can be used for riding and driving from the first day.

Before You Buy

A Mare, Gelding, or Stallion?

Basic questions like this one can be answered only in general terms because individual situations differ too much, and there are exceptions to any rule. The rule in this particular case would be: Geldings are reliable and even-tempered; mares are trusting, learn easily, and are generally of stable health but tend to be restless and unpredictable when in heat; stallions are spirited, temperamental, strong, and sometimes difficult. These sketchy descriptions can serve as a guideline for choosing a pony. Their implications are:
• An inexperienced pony enthusiast should choose a gelding.
• Someone who has a good sense for animals and treats them neither timidly nor roughly or someone who is interested in breeding ponies should thing about buying a mare.
• A stallion should be owned only by someone with extensive practical experience with horses. A stallion's primary purpose is to serve as a stud.

In addition to the qualities that go along with sex, each pony has typical breed characteristics and an individual personality of its own. These latter qualities can considerably modify the stereotype of the obedient gelding, the trusting mare, or the fiery stallion. I have seen geldings, for instance, that were full of temperament and more difficult to handle than many a stallion; and I have known mares whose serenity was unsurpassed and stallions that allowed themselves to be cared for, ridden, and harnessed to carts without the slightest objection.

A gelding is equal to a stallion in power and ability to exert himself. If you choose a stallion, you have to give some extra thought to how you are going to house him; that is, you have to have separate quarters and a separate pasture for him. Advice from an experienced pony person is extremely useful in this case.

Papers

Registration papers are essential for breeding within the context of a recognized breed association. A foal can be registered only if its dam is entered in the register of a breed society and if its sire is a registered stud.

To compete in classes or shows restricted to members of a breed, you must present proof that your pony is registered with that breed association. But to show in an open hunter show, dressage show, or combined training event, it will not be necessary to register your pony. Pony hunter classes are divided into small (under 12.2 hands), medium (12.2 to 13.2 hands), and large (13.2 to 14.2 hands) divisions. Most hunter shows are recognized with the American Horse Shows Association, from which you can get a "permanent card" that certifies your pony's eligibility for a specific division. To get one, have your pony measured by the show's official veterinarian and fill out an application.

Costs

If you are thinking of buying a pony, you will want to have some idea of the costs involved. How great is the initial investment—buying a pony, equipping it, possibly buying a pasture, building a barn or shelter—and what are the running costs of keeping a pony? You had best make a list on the basis of your own ideas and requirements.

For a family pony that is to be kept outside, the list could look something like this:
• Initial costs. The pony itself (preferably already trained), a saddle and saddle pad, girth, stirrup leathers and irons, crupper, bridle and bit (complete set), a halter, ropes, a horse blanket, grooming equipment, a riding helmet, rain gear, riding boots, a bucket, a shovel, and a pitch fork.

• Running expenses. Rent on a pasture or stall, grain and hay, bedding, items for routine care, worm medicines, vaccinations, veterinarian's and blacksmith's bills, and insurance.

If you study and compare prices for the individual items as charged by specialty stores, as advertised in horse magazines, and as cited by other pony owners, horse farms, or general farmers, you will notice that prices can vary widely. This is why no prices are listed here.

The most important item on the list of initial expenses is, of course, the pony itself. The price range for different kinds of ponies is huge, and it is therefore best to determine first exactly what qualities you want your pony to have and how it should look. You need to decide on breed (size), desired use, sex, age, and degree of training. Then you can compare the prices of the ponies that meet your criteria. An expensive pony is not always the best, but a registered animal that has done well in shows or a pony that has mastered more than the three basic gaits (page 62) does not come cheap. As a rule, small ponies cost less than larger ones; stallions that are not used for breeding, less than geldings; and geldings, often less than mares. A fully trained animal obviously is more expensive than one that has just been broken, and a pony that is broken costs more than a young, totally untrained one or a foal. But the price should not be the only determining factor. The ultimate decision should be based on the animal itself. It is unwise to try to save money on the initial outlay since the costs of keeping a pony—possibly over a very long period—are basically the same whether the animal is fully trained or unschooled or whether it is strong or weak.

The costs of keeping a pony depend on how it is quartered. Keeping a pony in a rented stall costs the most and is almost as expensive as keeping a full-size horse. Keeping it in an open shelter and a pasture year-round and looking after it yourself is obviously the least expensive way and is also the most satisfying solution.

Where Can You Find a Good Pony?

In recent years the variety of ponies you can buy has become very large, and yet it is not easy to find the right pony. After all, the one you choose should embody all the qualities you have settled on after extensive deliberation, and you also want an animal that you genuinely like. The situation is ideal if you are already acquainted with a pony and have ridden it—perhaps in a riding stable or on a pony farm—or if you are given the opportunity to keep the pony for a few days on trial to get to know it. Unfortunately, these opportunities are rare. But before you contemplate a more uncertain measure like putting an ad in the paper or going to a horse auction, you should consult the pony owners or breeders of your acquaintance. They may know of a good pony for sale that you would otherwise hear of too late. Time and patience are almost always the secret behind a lucky buy.

If you are looking for a healthy young animal to train yourself, you will find one most easily and with the least risk of disappointment by locating a breeder of well-known stock through a breed association (page 68). This way you will be more likely to get a well-bred and -raised pony than if you tried to buy your pony through an ad in your local paper or a specialized magazine. A purchase through a dealer is a private agreement between buyer and seller and always contains an element of chance because — except for a short trial ride — you will rarely have an opportunity to get to know the pony before you buy it. This is understandable because nobody likes to entrust his pony to a stranger for an extended trial period.

You have to take the seller's word and rely on your own observations if you buy your pony from a dealer and, even more so, if you go to a horse auction. But reputable dealers—and there are many in spite of the proverbial stories about dishonest ones—will not try to cheat you. The charm of a rural horse market, where the old custom of sealing a sale with a handshake still prevails, may easily tempt you to buy a pony on the spur of the moment; and it is quite possible to acquire a healthy, obedient pony this way. But there is also a chance that the spontaneously purchased animal will turn out to have ailments, flaws, or bad habits. If you hope to find a good pony at an auction, you should either be exceptionally knowledgeable yourself or take along an experienced horse person to advise you.

In this context I should like to mention that there is one other source of ponies, but making use of it requires an especially good instinct as well as knowledge and a big dose of luck. I am talking about buying a pony destined for slaughter. Many a good and basically healthy pony that has become a burden to its owner or was taken to the slaughterhouse on account of some passing illness has been saved this way. One such pony that was purchased for very little money won a jumping contest on the riding farm I mentioned above after its savior and new owner had worked with it and trained it for only a short time.

When You Buy

When you have found a pony you like—it may be love at first sight—you should remain calm and not rush into a purchase. The pony should be examined carefully and thoroughly by a veterinarian and tested for its qualities by a pony expert. Important factors are:

Handling

The pony (whether tied or in a pasture) should remain calm when you approach it. Stroke its back and loins, and touch its head or ears or lift up one of its legs. If you can observe the pony in a pasture, watch how it acts when it is caught. Is it friendly or wild? Carefully try catching it yourself. If the pony tries to get the better of you by evading you constantly, think twice before you buy it.

As to how the pony behaves at the blacksmith's, when being loaded and unloaded, and in road traffic, you generally have only the seller's word to go on. If you have any doubts, his statements should, for safety's sake, be put down in writing as part of the sale's agreement.

You can tell the age of a pony by the position of its incisor teeth. Left: teeth form an almost straight line, up to eleven years; middle: slanting teeth, twelve to seventeen years; right: angled teeth, over seventeen years.

Age

How valuable a pony is for its intended use and how much you will have to pay for it will depend to a considerable degree on its age. It is therefore very important to know exactly how old it is. If the pony has registration papers, its age will be entered there. If you have any reason to doubt the accuracy of the age given, you should check the pony's age yourself. This is not too easy. An active, lively

Before You Buy

pony may be twenty or more years old without showing it, and an inexperienced person is therefore unlikely to estimate a pony's age accurately. Age is determined by examining the degree of wear and the position of the teeth. If you do not have a horse expert with you to help you, there is a method that will give you at least some idea. Ask the dealer to expose the pony's teeth. Look at them in profile. The incisor teeth of a young pony meet to form an almost straight line. The older the pony, the more arch-shaped is the profile of the teeth and the more forward they point. The teeth of an old pony stand out almost horizontally.

Health

It is of utmost importance that the pony you buy be in perfect health. Although ponies are very robust and less subject to sickness than large horses, there are a number of diseases (page 50) that attack them. Have the animal you have chosen examined by a veterinarian before you sign the purchase agreement. If this is impossible because of time pressure or some other reason, look the pony over carefully yourself. Does it have cloudy or watery eyes or a discharge from the nose? Is it too thin, with a caved-in look? Is the position of the legs faulty, does it move stiffly, or — worse yet — is it lame? Is the hair of the coat and mane blunt-ended and rough? Check the hoofs with special care: Is there some deformity, deep furrow, or crack? If you notice any of these signs, you should delay the transaction until a veterinarian has determined their cause — which may be insignificant — or refrain from the purchase altogether.

One ailment that Icelandic ponies in particular are subject to is summer eczema (page 52). This is a skin disorder that is difficult — and in the fall and winter impossible — to detect and represents an additional reason for consulting a veterinarian before you buy.

Have your veterinarian check to make sure the pony doesn't suffer from heaves or any other respiratory problem, periodic ophthalmia (moonblindness), or any communicable disease. Once you have bought an unsound pony, you probably will neither be able to get your money back nor sell him again.

A Valid Sales Contract

Since buying a pony involves a considerable financial investment, it is best to prevent misunderstandings, misrepresentation of facts, and false promises by drawing up a well-thought-through, clearly formulated, written contract.

In addition to the identification of the parties concluding the agreement and the name and description of the pony (age, size, color, markings, ancestry), the contract should include the purchase price, conditions of transfer, specific responsibilities of the parties (for example, who is responsible for the transport of the animal), as well as a statement that the pony is free from the major common diseases. Specific qualities and skills the seller claims the pony to have should also be listed in the contract.

Necessary Insurance

Adequate insurance protection is in your own interest. In your capacity as owner of a pony, you should certainly take out liability insurance. Then, too, riders and the parents of children who ride should buy adequate liability insurance. Finally, with pony riding as with any sport, accident insurance is also essential.

Pony Breeds

Of the many different pony breeds that are found all over the world—many countries on the five major continents have breeds that are native there—I will describe here only those that are bred in our latitudes, that are suitable for leisure and sport use, and that are commonly available.

Connemara Pony *Photo on page 18*

Origin and Development of the Breed: The appearance of the elegant Connemara pony conforms completely to that of a typical saddle horse and gives little hint of its original type, a type that reflected the harsh living conditions of its homeland, Ireland. The wiry, hard-working Celtic ponies were the ancestors of the Connemara. The Celts had introduced them to Ireland in the fourth century B.C., and the ponies settled in the wild, lonely hills of the Connemara district in the western part of the island, which is still the home of their descendants. These ponies are the oldest breed of horses native to Ireland. In time they were crossed with Andalusians, Berbers, and later with Arabians and English Thoroughbreds, and in the process the qualities of the Connemara pony became more manifold. To the original hardiness, stamina, and resilience of its ancestors were added a more refined type, speed, and an exceptional talent for jumping. Since the beginning of this century, a greater consolidation of the breed has been pursued; and in 1923, the Connemara Pony Breeders' Society of Ireland was founded. The popularity and the distribution of this attractive, versatile pony have grown so much in the last few decades that these ponies are now raised in many countries. The success of some of the breeders has been so great—as in Holland, for instance—that their ponies are often considered equal to—and are sometimes preferred over—those from Ireland. In the Connemara district, the ponies are generally raised half wild, and they are therefore rugged and of an extremely stable constitution.

Appearance and Characteristics: The Connemara pony looks like an elegant small horse: a noble head carried high, with a broad forehead, and narrow toward the muzzle; large, intelligent eyes; ears that are not too small; a relatively long neck; a strong back with good saddle position; a muscular, slightly slanted croup; short, very muscular legs; and good, solid hoofs. Size: 13.0 to 14.2 hands (132 to 147 cm). The original dun color with contrasting dark mane and tail has unfortunately become uncommon. White, brown, and black are the colors most commonly seen today. What the friends of the Connemara most admire is the combination of typical pony traits—such as robustness, ruggedness, good health, stamina, frugality, and surefootedness—with attributes of light horse breeds: for example, the ease with which they carry the rider; long, smooth strides; and aptitude for jumping. In addition they are intelligent and courageous and have an agreeable disposition.

Aptitudes and Uses: The Connemara's performance in competitions is especially highly valued, and its enthusiasm for jumping has resulted in its becoming an excellent hunter. But the prime use of this pony —in Ireland as well as in the other countries where it is raised—is recreational riding. It is a reliable and docile riding pony that can carry adults and can be trusted, with proper supervision, to carry a child safely on its back.

Welsh Pony, Sections A, B, C, and D
Photos on page 28

Origin and Development of the Breed: Welsh ponies come, as their name implies, from Wales, the harshest and most mountainous part of Great Britain. Ponies and horses were used here from time immemorial for crossing difficult terrain, as pack animals, as herding ponies, and for tilling the soil.

In addition to the Welsh Mountain pony (the original breed), there is the imposing Welsh Cob— also a very old breed—as well as two more recent breeds.

The Welsh pony probably descended from the small and tough Celtic ponies. This versatile pony with great endurance is extremely popular in England and has many admirers in Germany and the United States as well. There are four different sections of Welsh ponies: Welsh Mountain pony is Section A; Welsh Riding pony is Section B; Welsh pony of the Cob type is Section C; Welsh Cob is Section D. The Welsh Pony and Cob Society formulated the standards for the four sections in 1902.

Pony Breeds

Welsh Mountain Pony, Section A

Appearance and Characteristics: This extremely pretty little pony—measuring up to 12 hands (122 cm)—looks like a miniature horse. The head is small, expressive, and aristocratic with large eyes, small pointed ears, delicate, wide nostrils, and a slightly dished foil. The body and legs are strong and sound; the hoofs, small and shapely; the mane and tail, fine and long. Welsh Mountain ponies come in all colors except skewbald (this is true of all Welsh ponies). The Welsh Mountain has a lively temperament, a good-natured disposition, a steady and light way of going, and a good aptitude for jumping. It is not very robust and therefore somewhat more complicated to keep than more primitive ponies.

Aptitudes and Uses: This is a good riding and pulling pony for children. (Caution is in order with individuals of very lively temperament.)

Welsh Riding Pony, Section B

Appearance and Characteristics: This light and elegant pony resembles the Welsh Mountain type but is somewhat larger, measuring up to 13.2 hands (137 cm). It is energetic and steady yet lively and of an agreeable disposition. It has excellent riding qualities and is a good jumper.

Aptitudes and Uses: This pony is extremely well suited for competing (but usually kept in a stable in this case). It is also good for recreational use and is a charming, talented, and intelligent riding pony for older children and adolescents.

Welsh Pony of the Cob Type, Section C

Appearance and Characteristics: This pony looks heavier and more powerful than the Welsh Riding pony, but it is of the same size (13.2 hands—137 cm). It is strong and compact, with sound legs. It has a lively temperament and is good-natured and hardy. Its gaits and pulling ability are excellent, and it likes to jump.

Aptitudes and Uses: A versatile pony for young people and adults, it is especially well suited for cross-country riding, pleasure riding, and hunting, as well as for pleasure driving.

Welsh Cob, Section D

Appearance and Characteristics: The term *cob* is used to describe a certain type of horse, namely, medium-size, strong animals that are suited for all kinds of riding. The Welsh Cob is a real weight carrier, powerful, stocky, and short-legged yet precise and quick as well. It has a noble head with very lively, slightly protruding eyes. The body is muscular, with pronounced withers, a round croup, strong legs, long, silky fetlock hair, and hard, well-shaped hoofs. Size: from 13.2 hands (137 cm) on up, without upper limit. Welsh Cobs are often taller than 14.2 hands (148 cm) but are still considered ponies. The Welsh Cob is tough, courageous, and steady as well as good-natured. It has an easygoing temperament and good instincts. It is also robust and easy to keep.

Aptitudes and Uses: This is a reliable horse for family use, suited for pleasure riding, dressage, jumping, and pleasure driving; it is also a spirited hunter. It can be ridden by children but can carry fairly heavy adults as well.

Shetland Pony

Photos on page 28 and on back cover

Origin and Development of the Breed: For many centuries, the life of Shetland ponies on their native ground—the Shetland Islands—has consisted of nothing but hard work and the struggle for survival in a harsh environment. Opinions differ on the breed's origin. All we can say for sure is that these ponies have lived for over 2,000 years on this group of islands northeast of the Scottish coast. The vegetation is very sparse; there are not even any trees. Hunger and cold have always been the main threats to these brave little horses in their native habitat. In their homeland they still live outdoors and are exposed to the elements. The human inhabitants of the Shetland Islands, fishermen and farmers, used to use them for riding, pulling carts, and carrying loads across difficult paths. They even sold the ponies for use in the mines in England. But the English discovered the pony's aptitude as a children's riding pony, and a great wave of exporting Shetlands to all parts of the world followed.

Shetland ponies, which had preserved their character despite some crossbreeding, now became the companions of children as riding or driving ponies. They are raised in innumerable countries.

Appearance and Characteristics: The head, which should not be too large, looks imposing with its broad forehead, expressive and intelligent eyes, and flaring nostrils. The very small ears peek out between the long, thick forelock and the rise of the mane. The neck is short and very strong, the back straight, and the croup well muscled. The sturdy little animals have short, strong legs and luxuriant manes and tails. The coat is short and smooth in the summer and longer and very dense in winter. The Shetland comes in all colors, including skewbald. The average size is about 10 hands (100 cm), with a minimum set at 9.2 hands (97 cm) and a maximum at 10.2 hands (107 cm). In relation to its size, the Shetland pony is probably the strongest of all horses. It is very well muscled, powerfully built, and has very sound bones, joints, and hoofs. Shetlands are tough, modest in their demands, and long lived, and they should be kept in the open. They are agile, and move with grace and ease. By temperament they are alert and quite lively; and, unless improperly treated, they are good natured.

Aptitudes and Uses: The Shetland pony makes a good riding pony for children (from around four to ten years old) and is especially well suited for driving. It is strong enough to pull even adults in a cart. In competition Shetlands display their speed and agility with great eagerness. At many pony farms they stand around patiently, waiting to give rides on their solid, broad backs to children who are spending their free time or vacations there. In Holland there is a Shetland pony park with 400 cottages on about 100 acres of land where families can spend their vacations and the children can romp around on 800 or so "Shetties." But Shetlands, the great favorites of children, should always be treated as playmates, never as toys.

Dartmoor Pony *Photo on page 28*

Origin and Development of the Breed: The Dartmoor is a close relative of the Exmoor pony and also lives in a harsh climate, namely, in the high moors of the southwestern tip of England. It belongs to an ancient, indigenous race of horses. The farmers of this region have used this pony exclusively for riding. But the Dartmoor is not without marks of foreign influence. In an effort to produce a strong but small pony for heavy work in mines, breeders in the last century introduced some Shetland blood. Later, in trying to return closer to the original type, they crossed the Dartmoor with English Thoroughbreds. In our time, only Dartmoor stock is used for breeding. There are a number of Dartmoor studs in countries other than England, the most noteworthy being Holland.

Appearance and Characteristics: The looks of the Dartmoor are pleasing and attractive: a good posture of the head, which is small and noble; a sturdy, well-muscled body and sound legs. The Dartmoor is a small, pretty riding pony, excellent in galloping, jumping, and elegant movements. Energy, stamina, and a sound constitution are the hall marks of this breed. Dartmoors come in almost all colors except skewbald. Their size is around 11.3 to 12.2 hands (120 to 127 cm). Of special importance are the characteristics that make it an ideal pony for children: It is goodnatured, willing, and absolutely reliable, and it is calm without every being boring. On the contrary, it shows a lively interest in what goes on and is eager and ambitious. It always likes children, no matter what the situation. Dartmoors can be kept outdoors.

Aptitudes and Uses: Because of its even temperament, excellent character, and comfortable gaits, the Dartmoor is especially desirable as a riding pony for children. Even very small children can, with proper supervision, be entrusted to it. It is also ideal for beginning riders. Since it is ambitious and likes to participate in everything, it is a good candidate for competitions. Since the Dartmoor likes to act the star at shows, it often is the favorite of the enthusiastic spectators.

Exmoor Pony *Photo on page 28*

Origin and Development of the Breed: The Exmoor pony is considered the prototype of a real pony. The original strain has remained quite pure because the ponies have lived throughout the ages in the wild and lonely landscape of Exmoor in southwest-

ern England. Today the Exmoor pony is kept half wild in its native region. It is a small, compact animal with enormous carrying strength. The qualities of this small pony are so outstanding that it has been used for crossbreeding in several breeds and even forms part of the original stock of the English Thoroughbred.

Appearance and Characteristics: Characteristic of this usually dun-colored pony are its whitish mouth and lips (the nostrils and nose are black). The dark eyes with their slightly drooping upper lids also have light rims. The pony is sturdy with a strong, medium-long back and short, strong legs with hard, little hoofs. The mane and tail are thick. In the summer, the coat is dense and smooth with a coppery sheen to it. In the cold season (winters in Exmoor are very severe), it is dull, rough, and shaggy though elastic, and it sheds water and snow. The pony's size is about 12.0 to 12.3 hands (122 to 130 cm). The Exmoor is one of the toughest ponies, sound as a bell, modest in its demands, quick, adroit, and surefooted. Its gaits are good, and it jumps well. Exmoors are famous for their intelligence and aptitude for learning, but some are not very trusting toward people and are almost shy.

Aptitudes and Uses: This is an excellent riding pony for children and adolescents.

New Forest Pony
Photos on pages 28 and 46

Origin and Development of the Breed: Anyone who is not familiar with this breed and sees a tiny, well-proportioned pony next to another elegant-looking one that is 2 hands (20 cm) taller will be amazed that both animals belong to the same breed. The reason for the difference between the two types lies in the origin and development of this pony. Its place of origin, as well as the most important center of breeding, is in New Forest, a former royal hunting estate in southern England. Here wild ponies have lived as far back as anyone can remember, and these ponies are believed to be the ancestors of the New Forest pony. When men began to till the land, the herd is said to have divided and each developed separately. In response to different conditions of climate and terrain, larger and smaller types developed within the breed. Another theory maintains that crossing with other breeds—including Arabians and English Thoroughbreds—gave rise to the variations among New Forest ponies. In the last fifty years, crosses with other breeds have been avoided, and the best qualities have been accentuated through careful breeding. Now that New Forest ponies, like most other pony breeds, are no longer used as work horses, the goal is to produce a good, versatile riding pony. Herds of mares and selected studs roam year-round in a large, enclosed area of New Forest. Outside this original territory of the New Forest pony there are many private studs. But the attractive "New Forester" has acquired a large following way beyond the borders of Great Britain for its qualities as a light riding pony. The most important breeding center outside of England is Holland, where New Forest ponies of excellent quality are raised.

Appearance and Characteristics: The smaller type of the New Forest pony looks more compact and "ponylike" than the larger one, but it is held in especially high esteem by breeders. It measures about 11.3 to 13.0 hands (120 to 132 cm); and its "big brother," 13.0 to 14.1 hands (132 to 147 cm). Both types are characterized by their proud carriage and the intelligent look of their eyes. The head is narrow and betrays some Arab influence. The neck is short and strong, the withers fairly prominent, and the back strong and relatively long. The narrow croup is steep, and the legs are muscular and healthy. Brown is the dominant color, varying in shade to the deepest black. New Forest ponies have a healthy constitution; they are trusting and friendly and learn easily. They are good natured and have a lively temperament. Their gaits are flowing and cover a lot of ground, and these ponies are good jumpers.

Aptitudes and Uses: The New Forest pony, too, is versatile for pleasure or competitive riding. It is used in horsemanship and hunter competitions, in dressage, and in eventing (tests of dressage, cross-country, and show jumping). In England, it is used for racing as well. The small type of New Forester is a popular mount for children (though not always easy to ride on account of its temperament), and the larger one is a suitable riding pony for older children and light adults. New Forest ponies are somewhat more demanding to keep than the extremely robust breeds.

Pony Breeds

Camargue Pony

Origin and Development of the Breed: This breed, also known under the names Camarguais and Crin Blanc (white mane), has lived since time immemorial in the strange landscape of the Camargue, a marshy island in southern France in the Rhône delta. Life in this wild region has kept the type of this horse the same despite repeated introductions of Iberian, Arab, and Berber blood, a type that still characterizes today's Camargue pony. Ridden expertly by the *gardian,* or cowboy, this pony drives the half-wild black Camargue bulls and separates them from the herd. For riding, stallions are used almost exclusively. The mares serve only for breeding. The breeders are the *manadiers,* owners of large herds of horses and fighting bulls. In recent times their breeding efforts have been aimed at producing a somewhat larger and more broadly built Camarguais without sacrificing any of its hardiness, enthusiasm, or fiery temperament.

Appearance and Characteristics: The Camargue pony is wiry and tough. Its size is 13.1 to 14.1 hands (135 to 145 cm). Typical of this breed is a rather heavy head, often with a Roman nose and with pronounced jaws, small ears, and lively eyes that express intelligence. The neck is short and strong, with a full mane. The back is muscular, the croup usually steep. The legs are muscular and strong, the hoofs wide and hard. Like all white horses, the Camargue pony is born black. The fine, thick coat, which is long and shaggy in wintertime, turns "white like the salt of the steppes" only when the pony is five or six years old. Excellent instincts, intelligence, and a lively temperament are characteristic of the Camargue pony. It is energetic and persevering, hardy, and modest in its demands. Its movements.are controlled and adroit. A crisp walk and a swift or short-strided gallop are its main gaits.

Aptitudes and Uses: Until recently the Camargue pony was used solely for herding. It is only since recreational riding, especially cross-country, has become so popular in France that the Camarguais has been used as a riding pony for vacationers. The demand for this pony—outside of France as well—has grown so much that it greatly exceeds the supply. An important factor in the development of its characteristic qualities is that the Camargue pony be trained in its traditional manner and that it be ridden, as far as possible, the way the *gardians* do with their traditional saddles and bridles. In France, a somewhat different saddle is used for cross-country riding. Anyone who has a chance to ride a Camargue stallion will feel right away that he has a spirited, strong, attentive, highly responsive, and extremely maneuverable pony under the saddle. The Camarguais is less suited for children than for adults, whom it carries easily and without tiring.

Haflinger
Photos on page 55 and on back cover

Origin and Development of the Breed: The southern Tirol is the Haflinger's original home. According to old sources, a "race of small mountain horses" existed as early as the Middle Ages in the Rhaetian Alps near Merano and Bolzano. The origin of these small horses that were used by the local people as pack animals and for riding on this difficult terrain is not clear. The first registered Haflinger stallion, a bay named "249 Folie," was descended on the paternal side from a famous Arabian stallion. The birth and registration of 249 Folie in 1874 marked the beginning of systematic breeding of Haflingers in the southern Tirol, then part of Austria. Since that time the breeding goals have changed along with the tasks for which the pony was intended; and, as a consequence, the compact, small work horse has been transformed into a light, elegant animal with a long stride. Today, Haflingers are used primarily for leisure activities, although they are still employed quite extensively in farming and lumbering as well. When the southern Tirol became part of Italy after World War I, the breeding centers moved to the northern Tirol, where the production of purebred Haflingers is now intensively pursued through strictly selective breeding. The pony farm of Ebbs near Kufstein (with an exemplary stud) has attached to it a lodging center for riders and a riding and driving school. Haflingers are now bred all over the world, and the small "blond horse" has made an excellent adjustment to different climates and conditions in places as varied as the United States, Brazil, South

Pony Breeds

Africa, and northern India. Haflingers are also bred in many European countries such as France, Holland, and even in the original pony country, Great Britain. This pony is also very popular in the Federal Republic of Germany. The stud farms in Bavaria (since 1935) and in Westphalia are the most famous. Here, some strains include crossings with Arabians to improve the riding quality of the ponies, but in order to keep its type, the Haflinger should not have too much Arabian blood.

Appearance and Characteristics: The appearance of the Haflinger is unmistakable: chestnut (light, red, or dark chestnut) with a very light, thick mane and tail. The pony looks compact and well muscled. The short, muscular head is finely modeled (not thick or pudgy) with a broad forehead; large, lively eyes; small, mobile ears; and a slightly concave or dished nose. The head has an expressive and quite aristocratic look. The neck is well placed, the withers not at all prominent, that is, too flat. The legs are muscular, the hoofs healthy and hard. Size: 13.1 to 14.1 hands (135 to 145 cm).

Haflingers are not demanding to keep, since they are light eaters and are healthy and resistant to disease. They have an excellent character and a quiet disposition.

Aptitudes and Uses: Because of its surefootedness and hardiness, the Haflinger is especially suited for use in difficult terrain. It feels at home in the mountains, even when there is snow and ice. Its good nature makes it an ideal mount for beginning riders, and with its calm temperament, a reliable partner for children's vaulting. The Haflinger's uses are manifold: It is a good family and leisure-time pony that can be ridden on long and short excursions and vacation tours and can pull sleds or skiers in the winter. It also does well in the area of sports as a school horse, in dressage, and even in jumping. It performs willingly both under a saddle and in harness. At rural festivals and parades, farmers display their teams with justified pride, and the sleek Haflingers seem to share their pride as they parade in their richly ornamented harnesses.

Fjord Pony
Photos on pages 17 and 27

Origin and Development of the Breed: The Fjording, as it is called in its native Norway, belongs to an ancient race. The Vikings used it in their warring expeditions both to cover long distances and in actual combat. These small horses were carried across the seas as far as Iceland and thus are among the ancestors of the Icelandic pony (page 22). The Fjordings were the farmers' indispensible helpers, and these mountain ponies were bred to become strong and heavy little work horses. Their use was confined to Norway until around 1900. Then the Danes became interested in this vigorous and robust animal, and Denmark became the prime area where it was bred. After World War II, it was introduced into northern Germany, the Rhineland, and Hesse for agricultural work. Since utility horses have been replaced more and more by motorization, the Fjording has lost its economic importance, and recent breeding efforts have been aimed at making a riding pony of it.

Appearance and Characteristics: The breed characteristics of the Fjord pony are so obvious that this pony is immediately recognizable. Its special features are its dun coloration; the stiff, trimmed, bicolored mane; and the dorsal stripe, or eel mark, running from the top of the head down the neck and back to the tail. There are six color variations:
• Brown dun: light brown, brown, and dark brown dun; black dorsal stripe; light mane and tail.
• Red dun: light red, red, and dark red dun; a not very strongly marked reddish brown dorsal stripe; mane and tail have a reddish tint.
• Light dun: light with a black dorsal stripe.
• Yellow dun: light with a reddish brown dorsal stripe.
• Gray Dun: ranging from light to very dark gray; black dorsal stripe.
• White: white all over with a faint yellowish dorsal stripe.

If the mane is bicolored, the outer, light hair is cut about 1 inch (2 to 3 cm) shorter than the black middle stripe. The Norwegians trim the mane evenly. Its rounded shapes give the Fjord pony a compact and sturdy look. The head is muscular with a broad, flat forehead; large, intelligent eyes; a

21

Pony Breeds

slightly dish-shaped nose; and small, widely spaced ears. The short neck is strong and very muscular, the withers, not very pronounced. The back should not be too short. The legs are powerful; the hoofs are healthy and grow fast. Size: 13.1 to 14.1 hands (135 to 145 cm).

The Fjord pony matures slowly, and is not fully grown until five years. Its sturdy build gives no indication of the dexterity, nimbleness, and accuracy of its movements. This pony has a lively and pleasant disposition and is robust and good-natured but also sensitive. It has kept its instincts and has an excellent sense of orientation. Like most ponies, it is a light eater, fertile, and long lived. Its modest demands and hardiness make it a relatively unproblematic animal to keep.

Aptitudes and Uses: Since the Fjord pony is strong enough to carry even a moderately heavy person, it is ideal for the whole family. It is also temperamentally suited for riding, but its size and sometimes rather spirited disposition have to be taken into account when this pony is to be ridden by children with little experience in horsemanship. No special precautions are necessary, of course, if the children ride under supervision on a pony farm or in a riding school. Fjord ponies are good for vaulting and are also employed in the therapy of disabled persons. Their reliability and their broad backs are extremely valuable for this difficult task. With its background as a utility horse and its pulling power, the Fjord pony also performs well when harnessed. Its versatility, the simplicity of its care, and its cheerful and agreeable nature have won the Fjording friends all over the world.

Icelandic Pony *Photo on inside front cover*

Origin and Development of the Breed: The Icelandic pony has been bred for over a thousand years on the wild and remote island of Iceland near the Arctic Circle. The Normans, or Vikings, who began settling "Ice Land" in the late ninth century brought their horses, ancestors of the Fjord ponies, along with them. To protect their healthy and hardy stock from diseases that might be introduced from foreign countries, the popular assembly (the Icelandic *thing*) passed a decree in the mid-tenth century,

barring the entry of all horses to the island. Apart, possibly, from size, today's Icelandic pony therefore resembles what the Viking horses must have looked like centuries ago.

No effort was made to promote this breed systematically until this century. Today its qualities are appreciated not only in Europe but all over the world.

Appearance and Characteristics: The Icelandic pony is of an extremely robust and compact type. The lively, slightly slanted eyes, the long, busy forelock, and the small ears give the powerful, wedge-shaped head the typical expression of natural charm that is characteristic of this breed. The firmly anchored teeth and the digestive system are adapted to dealing with and extracting food value from hard food, such as roots, and even frozen food. The neck is short and solid, the rump long, the short back well muscled, and croup steep. The legs are short and strong, the hips wide. The hair of the mane is thick and the tail long. The coat is made up of thick, coarse hair that is short in the summer and that gets long and stringy in the winter, shedding water and snow through a fine, wooly undercoat with longer cover hair. The coloration is varied, ranging from mouse grey to chestnut—the most common color—to brown and black, sometimes with a dorsal stripe and often with a blaze. The original qualities of this pony—resistance to disease, frugality, stamina, unfailing surefootedness, and a good mastery of swimming—were the results of adapting to harsh environmental conditions. The breed has preserved these qualities. It is not a finicky eater and tends to plumpness when kept on a good pasture. It can be kept in the open air (pasture with an open shed) all year round. Icelandic ponies are hardy and healthy except for a skin disease (summer eczema) that often afflicts them. They grow quite old and can, if properly kept, be ridden past the age of twenty. Icelandic ponies mature slowly, and preliminary training—getting them used to saddle and harness—cannot be initiated until they are four and a half years old. At five years they can be trained with a saddle, and when they have reached six, they can be ridden. Keeping them is unproblematical.

Icelandic ponies have a swift and long stride, and they can move with astonishing speed. They have

Pony Breeds

one advantage over most other pony and horse breeds: a talent, inherited from their wild ancestors, for being more than three-gaited. In addition to the three basic gaits—walk, trot, and canter—the Icelandic pony easily masters the running walk and often paces as well (page 62). Every Icelandic pony is born with an aptitude for the running walk, and the first few days of its life will show whether or not a particular pony will use this gait instinctively. If a pony has the aptitude for this gait but cannot actually perform it, it can later be taught by someone with patience and a good understanding of the principles involved. To do this, you will need the help of an experienced trainer.

Icelandic ponies range in size from 12.1 to 14.1 hands (125 to 145 cm). They are basically docile and good natured. A lively breed, they sometimes tend to be temperamental, a quality that is considered desirable by Icelandic horseback riders and that is a positive goal in Icelandic breeding efforts.

Aptitudes and Uses: The talents of the Icelandic pony are varied. In Germany it is kept almost exclusively for recreational use. In its land of origin and on other continents, it is still employed in agricultural work and lumbering. Its toughness, stamina, and thriftiness make it ideal for long-distance riding as well as for extended excursions of pleasure riding, for which the running walk proves especially useful because it is so easy on the rider. These gallant little horses are strong enough to carry an adult rider across great distances of difficult terrain. Despite its relatively small size, the Icelandic pony is not necessarily the best choice for a child. Mastering this spirited mount can prove a challenging task indeed for children as well as for novice adult riders. On pony farms in Iceland, these diligent, light-footed little horses have proved very satisfactory for children and adults both in the ring and on the trail rides. The Icelandic pony is not a race horse in the usual sense of the word, but it will participate with spirit and courage in breakneck races in pacing and the running walk. There are regional, national, and international competitions for Icelandic ponies. The proud stance and upright posture of a well-schooled Iceland pony express both character and nobility.

German Riding Pony

Origin and Development of the Breed: The German Riding pony is not, properly speaking, a separate breed, but rather a strain resulting from the crossing of ponies and normal-size horses. This is why there is no point in discussing its early history. The idea of such a crossing originated in England, and the aim was to create a riding pony for young adults that could rival the performance of large horses in sports but that preserved the cooperative nature, resilience, steadiness, and surefootedness of the pony. For this reason pony mares were mated with English Thoroughbreds and Arabians, and the British Riding pony was created, a strain that was greeted with enthusiasm and became popular not only in Great Britain but that also became the model of similar efforts all over Europe and in the United States. In England, only crosses between ponies and thoroughbred horses are called riding ponies, whereas in Germany, crossings between different pony breeds are also categorized as German Riding ponies.

Appearance and Characteristics: The German Riding pony should look aristocratic. It should resemble a horse more than a typical pony. Its glossy coat of fine short hair gives it an elegant appearance. The traditional and valuable pony qualities, especially hardiness, modesty of demands, and resilience, are often lost, and the German Riding pony has to be kept in a stable. It is also closer to a full-size horse than a pony in temperament and way of going. It is characterized by long, elegant movements and good jumping ability, and its temperament is lively and sometimes rather difficult.

Aptitudes and Uses: This is exclusively a riding pony for young adults with riding experience; it is suited for competitions and eventing.

Pony of the Americas *Photo on page 17*

Origin and Development of the Breed: Not until 1954 had a western pony breed been developed in the United States for a particular purpose. The development of the Pony of the Americas breed is the outgrowth of a study made by Leslie L. Boomhower, a Mason City, Iowa, attorney who had acquired an Appaloosa horse mare and her colt. The sire of this foal had been a Shetland pony stallion. Mr. Boomhower was particularly impressed with the characteristics of this offspring, now known as Black Hand No. 1.

Appearance and Characteristics: The official breed registry for Appaloosa-colored ponies is from 46 to 54 inches in height. The coloring is characteristic of the Appaloosa horse, and the eye is encircled with white like a human's. The skin is mottled with an irregular spotting of black and white; this is especially noticeable about the nostrils. The hoofs are striped vertically black and white. Coat patterns vary. Most will be white over the loins and hips with dark round egg-shaped spots. These spots may vary in size from tiny specks to spots 4 inches in diameter. Some carry the spotting all over the body, but it is usually dominant over the hips. No two POAs will have identical markings. The POA is not only colorful, but also a rugged athlete built for speed and action.

Aptitudes and Uses: Because the POA is not too big and not too small, it is an excellent mount for youths. The breed standard calls for conformation between that of the Quarter horse and the Arabian horse, combining the superior characteristics of both, with the addition of Appaloosa coloration and characteristics.

Bosnian Mountain Pony *(Bosniake)*
Photo on page 17

Origin and Development of the Breed: The Bosnian Mountain pony is the descendant of an ancient race that had some blood of the wild horse breeds Tarpan and Przewalski. The Bosnian Mountain pony is a small, unprepossessing, tough pony that was used for centuries in the wild Bosnian (Yugoslavia) mountains and proved indispensible as a pack animal. During the Middle Ages the horses of the Turkish invaders left an Oriental stamp on the Bosnian Mountain pony that is still apparent today (though there were also later crossings). In Yugoslavia the Bosnian Mountain pony is still used as a pack animal as well as for riding and driving.

Appearance and Characteristics: The Bosnian Mountain pony is quite varied in size, ranging from 12.1 to 13.3 hands (125 to 140 cm). The head with its large, alert eyes looks noble. A strong neck and a short, sturdy back are characteristic of the breed. The withers are only slightly prominent, and the croup is steep. The legs are sound and muscular, and the healthy hoofs are hard as rocks. Colors: primarily dark browns, but also white and other colors. This extremely healthy and long-lived pony combines many good qualities. It is intelligent, willing, and eager to learn but at the same time full of temperament. Its surefootedness and strength for carrying are outstanding. In spite of its relatively small size it carries adult riders. Its gaits are springy, and it often has an innate aptitude for the running walk and for pacing.

Aptitudes and Uses: This is a talented pony both under saddle and in harness, especially for children and young adults. Because of its staying power and modest demands (it is a light eater), it is well suited for long-distance pleasure riding. Children are especially fond of it because of its devoted attachment and loyalty to people.

Huzule Pony

Origin and Development of the Breed: The Huzule, too, is a descendant of the wild Tarpan. As in the case of the Bosnian Mountain pony, blood of Przewalski's horse and, later, Arabian blood were introduced into the race. The Huzule originated in the Carpathian mountains where it lived under the harshest of conditions and was used as a pack animal. Today it, too, is used as a riding pony. The main countries where Huzule ponies are raised and used are Rumania, Poland, Hungary, and Czechoslovakia.

Appearance and Characteristics: This strong pony has a handsome, quite noble-looking head, a relatively short back, a broad round croup, muscular legs, and small, hard hoofs. It measures about 13.1 to 13.3 hands (135 to 140 cm). The colors are dun, chestnut, and dark brown. Like all mountain horses, the Huzule pony is surefooted, tough, steady, and very modest in its demands. It has an even temperament, is extremely healthy, and is very easy to handle.

Aptitudes and Uses: The Huzule is still used as a

utility horse in its native countries, but because of its agreeable nature and modest demands it is also a good candidate for recreational use. It is suited for driving.

Dülmen and Arenberg-Nordkirchen
Ponies *Photos on pages 17 and 18*

Origin and Development of the Breeds: Germany is the only country on the European continent with a herd of wild horses that we know has not interbred with other horses for over 600 years. In the Merfelt Bruch near the Westphalian city of Dülmen a herd of small, indigenous horses has been living since at least 1316, when they are first mentioned in a contemporary document. These are the last horses in Germany that still live wild, and they represent the only German pony breed. Since the last century, the Dülmen horses have been under the ownership of the Dukes of Croy, to whom we owe the preservation and supervision of the breed. The herd of about 200 lives outdoors all year round under wild conditions. To maintain the hardiness, health, and resilience of the original breed, stallions of primitive type, such as Exmoors or Koniks (an extremely sound Polish pony breed) are introduced as studs.

Once a year, on the last Saturday in May, an event takes place that has become something of a popular festival. The yearling colts are separated from the rest of the herd and driven into an arena where they are branded. Only the very best are released back to the herd, and the rest are auctioned off. Mares are never sold. They spend their whole lives in the wild. The crossing of Dülmen stallions with Panje mares (*Panje* is a collective term for East European ponies) resulted over fifty years ago in a second herd of wild German ponies. The Duke of Arenberg in Nordkirchen, near Münster, started breeding these ponies, and today's Arenberg-Nordkirchen conform to the modern type of riding pony. They resemble the Dülmen horses but are somewhat larger and more elegant, serving as riding ponies for children and adolescents.

Appearance and Characteristics: The attractive Arenberg-Nordkirchen ponies have a very expressive head, alert dark eyes, a beautiful long mane, a relatively short neck, and a strong back. The croup is somewhat slanted, the legs muscular, and the hoofs small and healthy. The size is around 11.3 to 13.1 hands (120 to 135 cm). The most common colors are mouse gray, dun (with dorsal stripe and often a lateral marking), and dark brown (with light muzzle). Chestnut and black occur with less frequency. These healthy, resilient ponies are intelligent and spirited. They are good natured, move with elegance, and have a talent for galloping and for jumping.

Aptitudes and Uses: These friendly ponies are relatively uncomplicated to keep and thrive in the open air. If they are meant to participate in competition, they are usually kept in a stable. They are suited for dressage as well as for jumping, and they have proved reliable and attentive in vaulting.

Falabella Miniature Horse
Photo on back cover

The miniature horses that came into fashion a few years ago are very different from ponies. They are meant exclusively as pets and have none of the qualities of a horse or pony. The Argentinian J. C. Falabella first bred these miniature animals, but there are now other breeders, primarily in the United States and in Canada but also in England and in Germany. The smallest of these ponies grow to no more than about 4 hands (40 cm).

Housing Your Pony

Quarters have to be chosen in accordance with a pony's breed. Housing is the basic element on which the pony's health and well-being depend. These, in turn, affect its behavior and performance. Every pony that is put to use by people needs some sort of shelter, whether it be an open structure or an enclosed barn or stable. The ideal setup is a stable opening directly onto a paddock and a pasture, for every pony needs to graze, to be exposed to air, sun, rain, and wind, and to have lots and lots of exercise.

The Enclosed Barn

Ponies that are not suited for living outdoors because of their constitution or that are meant to participate in competitions need an enclosed barn or a stall in a barn or outbuilding. Because of the cruelty to the animal involved, a pony should never be kept in a standing stall (a narrow compartment where the tied animal is forced to stand). The stall for a small pony should measure at least 8 by 8 feet (2.5 by 2.5 m); larger ponies should have a space of about 10 by 12 feet (3 by 4 m) to be able to move around and lie down comfortably. (If several ponies live communally in a barn not divided with stalls, 7 by 8 feet (2.2 by 2.5 m) per animal is sufficient for smaller ponies and 10 by 10 feet (3 by 3m) for larger ones.)

Stalls should be constructed in such a manner that the ponies are able to look out. Doors leading outside should be made in two parts so that the upper half can be opened with the lower half closed. Ponies want to know what is going on around them. It relieves the monotony of living in a stable. There is nothing worse for these lively creatures than to be condemned to live day in and day out, perhaps for years on end, in a tight, dark, and musty space. Such "solitary confinement"

must not be tolerated! We have to make our ponies' homes as healthy and pleasant as possible. Daylight and fresh air are essential, and a window is therefore a must. In the case of very lively ponies or stallions that rear, reasons of safety suggest that the window be located about one foot above the pony's head. Windows that are lower should be made of glass-enclosed wire mesh or be protected by bars or mesh (make sure there is nothing the pony can injure itself on!). The stall should never be drafty (do not keep doors and windows open simultaneously for any length of time in cold weather). A pony that spends many hours standing in one place is more threatened by drafts than one that is exposed to rain and wind outside. The floor of the stall must be dry and as nonskid as possible. It should be at a slight grade so that liquids will run off. (Moist floors are cold, cause the bedding to get soggy, and are unhealthy for the pony.)

Feeding troughs and waterers should be at a level where the pony can reach them without contortions. The trough should be deep and wide enough so that the pony does not spill the feed while eating. Hay racks keep the hay from being scattered all over, but they have the disadvantage that minute particles of hay and dust fall down when the pony yanks out the hay, and these can irritate the pony's respiratory system. All troughs and buckets should be easy to clean. Automatic waterers should be located as far from the feeding trough as possible so that they do not get contaminated with bits of feed. Since ponies are very clever at opening the doors of their boxes, bolts or locks should be secure and out of the pony's reach.

Right: a Fjord stallion—his stance is a good indication of ▷ the undiminished strength of this old breed.

You will need a room for storing feed, bedding, tack, grooming items, and tools, and there should be an especially clean corner for the stable medicine cabinet. You need a sturdy stand for the saddle and bridle and a shelf with hooks for cleaning and grooming materials. If you are handy with tools you can build much of this yourself. Two-by-fours, boards (finished on the side that faces the pony's stall), and plywood can be used to construct compartments for feed and bedding. But they have to be built solidly so that they will not collapse at the first kick.

If these guidelines are followed and if we see to it that our pony gets plenty of exercise and regular food and care, an enclosed barn provides adequate housing. But for a robust pony enclosed quarters should never be more than a temporary solution.

The Open Barn with Paddock

The quarters that are most in keeping with a pony's nature are open barns—that is, shelters that open onto a paddock and, ideally, onto a pasture as well.

The Open Barn

An open shelter is particularly well suited for keeping several ponies. Of course, it has to be of an appropriate size. You should figure on about 10 by 10 feet (3 by 3 m) per pony. In addition, you will probably want a room for feed, bedding, and equipment.

Model for an open shelter for ponies. The resting area has two entry ways (left). The eating area (right) and the immediate surroundings of the shelter have a solid floor. This shelter provides a comfortable home for a pony.

Housing Your Pony

If there is enough space and you have plenty of building materials, a separate shed can be built for feeding. This way, the ponies' rest is less disturbed and the hay does not get absorbed in the bedding because the feeding shed is kept free of bedding and preferably has a hard-surfaced floor. Depending on the size of the structure, a building permit may be needed for it. Consult local authorities; regulations vary. Before you embark on building a shelter for your ponies, make sure you have legal permission to build on the space you have chosen.

Open shelters are usually built of wood, which is the most suitable material for this purpose. Whatever is used, the shelter must be solidly constructed, with three side walls that will keep out wind and rain completely. The fourth side is left partially or completely open. It should face away from prevailing winds to offer the pony proper protection. But there should always be a way of blocking off the open side (with a door) for when a pony is overheated or ill or has to be kept inside the shelter for some other reason. On the open side the roof should project 3 to 5 feet (1 to 1.5 m) beyond the floor so that rain and snow are kept out in the winter and the ponies have plenty of shade in the summer. The roof should be absolutely tight and be equipped with a gutter. To keep the rain water from the roof from making the ground soggy (in case there is no drainage pipe) a low barrel or a wood or stone drinking trough can be placed where the water drains off the roof. When choosing the site it is important to take the nature of the soil into account. The chosen spot should obviously be as dry as possible. This makes it much easier to build a good floor. A floor may consist of clay or sand (with a layer of gravel below it). The eating area and the area under the projecting roof can be covered with planking or bricks.

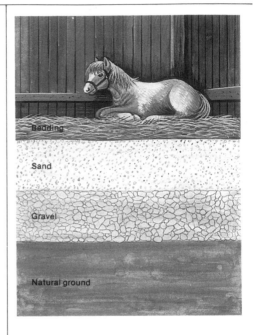

Construction of the floor for the resting area in an open shelter. The natural ground is covered with a layer of gravel (6 to 12 inches [15 to 30 cm]) and sand (8 to 12 inches [20 to 30 cm]). On top of this comes the bedding.

The floor of the barn (preferably somewhat higher than the ground) should be dry, warm, and not too hard. Cement floors are therefore not very suitable. If the open side of the shelter is partially closed off, the entry section must be wide enough that the ponies do not have to crowd and shove to get in—that is, it should be about 6½ feet (2 m) wide. Whether stalls (with walls about as high as the ponies' backs) are necessary within the shelter depends on how well the ponies get along, particularly at feeding time. The hay rack and feeding trough are mounted on the back wall

Housing Your Pony

but not one directly over the other. They should be of adequate width for all the ponies to eat. If a water line is on the premises or can be installed, automatic waterers are very practical (insulate the pipes for winter!). Open shelters can be constructed with many variations in floor plan, execution, and arrangement. Apart from the physical aspects of the site, the climate and the disposition of the ponies in question are the major influencing factors. And often actual experience will dictate changes until ''everything works'' and the ponies adopt their barn happily. Needless to say, consideration of the ponies' natural needs should be paramount, but we should also see to it that the quarters appear attractive and make a pleasant home.

Paddock

The more spacious the area in which the ponies spend most of their time, the more comfortable they will be. They need enough room to move about freely and to tussle and play with each other. I have repeatedly observed that ponies confined to too small a paddock spend excessive amounts of time standing around motionlessly in a doze. The fence — a paddock must, of course, be fenced in (page 37) — infringes on their need to move about. The area of a paddock should be at least 600 square feet (60 m²) and be in the shape of a long rectangle. A square does not provide enough length for running. The ground of the paddock gets very hard use from the ponies and will quickly turn into deep mire after hard rains or when the snow melts. This is extremely unhealthy for the hoofs and legs of the ponies—not to mention how filthy the coat gets. The ground of the paddock should therefore either be macadamized so that the water will run off or— and this is done more commonly—covered with a layer of sand that will absorb the water.

Constructing a foundation for the entire paddock the way it is done for the feeding area and the area under the protruding roof is very expensive and therefore usually feasible only for very small paddocks. Such a foundation must be built up properly by spreading sand, preferably on layers of gravel and crushed stone so the sand will not gradually be absorbed by the soil. If the ground is not naturally well drained, install drainage pipes to prevent the buildup of water.

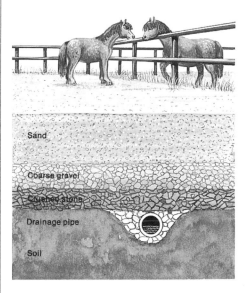

Sand

Coarse gravel

Crushed stone

Drainage pipe

Soil

Foundation of the paddock. The earth is covered with about 4 inches (10 cm) of crushed stone, 6 inches (15 cm) of coarse gravel, and 12 inches (30 cm) of sand. If the soil does not drain well, drainage pipes are installed.

Care and Grooming

Before you bring your pony home you should find out all you can (ideally from its previous owner) about how it was kept. This will help you understand and interpret its behavior and treat it accordingly. Also ask for the dates of past vaccinations and wormings and enter them in a pony record book. Place a photocopy of the pony's registration certificate in the front of the book if the pony has papers. Keep records of when your pony is shod, vaccinated, and wormed, the onset and course of illnesses, participation in competitions and long-distance trail rides, and any other important events in the life of your pony. Be sure not to neglect dates for further innoculations and wormings; it is essential for the pony's health that these procedures be attended to regularly. If your veterinarian has not yet had a chance to look the animal over, be sure to make up for this as soon as the pony has had a chance to get used to its new home. Have its teeth checked. Sharp edges on the molars caused by uneven wearing of the teeth can be filed down by the vet with a tooth rasp. If they are not taken care of they can cause injury to the tongue and gums, and they can be responsible for decreased food intake, digestive upsets, emaciation, and colic. The hoofs, too, have to be examined and trimmed or shod as needed (page 41).

Accustoming Your Pony to Its New Home

Ponies are very alert animals. They are conscious of the world they live in and get used to everything: the pasture, the barn, the people who look after them, other ponies, food and times of feeding, and all the sounds and smells of their surroundings. When there is a radical change in their lives, such as changing owners and homes, they are bound to react. Depending on the breed and the character of a given pony, this reaction may take the form of fear, shyness, and skittishness or curiosity and sometimes even aggressive behavior. Some ponies will pine and will therefore seem passive and apathetic. In such a case it is not easy to establish a trusting relationship. Too much activity, such as shouting, continual petting, and frequent feeding, does not help the pony. It wants to have a chance to explore its new surroundings peacefully by itself, and that takes time. On the other hand, it should not feel abandoned if it was used to living with others of its kind and is now to be kept by itself. The best way to win its confidence is to treat it with gentle friendliness. The children's joy and excitement over their new companion therefore has to be toned down a little during the first days, especially if the pony has not been used to children. It is best to make this clear to the children before the pony's arrival. If you have a proper setup for the pony, it does not usually take long before it begins to feel comfortable in its new home. The situation is somewhat more tricky if the newcomer is introduced into a pasture or a communal stable with other ponies where it has to find its own place in the already established rank. There is no telling in advance how "the new one" will be treated. Playful scuffling indicates that the newcomer has been accepted. But if there are serious fights, the introduction has to proceed more slowly, step by step. The ponies are placed together only for a short period at a time, and they are fed separately at the beginning. If the newcomer remains unaccepted after a period of getting acquainted, it has to be quartered separately in a stall or separate pasture. Luckily, such total incompatibility is rare among ponies.

I found out many years ago when I was still inexperienced with ponies how easy it is to do the wrong thing when trying especially hard to

Care and Grooming

please. We "found" our first pony on a narrow strip of grass by the roadside. It was tied very short and looked terrible, emaciated, and unkempt. Wanting to improve its miserable existence, we bought it, moved it to our pasture, cleaned it gently, fed it, and left it there a few days so it could recover. That is just what it did. It soon looked lively; its eyes and coat shone. One evening we brought it home where we had made a well-built, tall, and spacious shed ready for it. Food and water were set out. Petisa, as we called the pony mare, let herself be led into her stall and immediately began to eat. We left her alone and closed the large double-winged door, which was, however, not equipped with a lock. I had just fallen asleep when I was roused by a loud banging and crashing. It was our solicitously housed Petisa. She had managed to open the door by pushing and kicking it and had escaped from her unaccustomed confinement. Now she stood contentedly under the star-studded sky munching on some grass. She never again set foot in the shed because she was used to living without a roof over her head.

Problems of a Single Pony

What creature likes to live alone? From the small ant to the large elephant, almost all live in communities, herds, packs, colonies, or swarms. The community, whether large or small, offers protection, strength, and challenge. It gives them a place and a task. This is true for ponies, too. As soon as a pony is separated from the herd, it is deprived of an important part of its natural way of being, and it will always long for others of its kind. It has often happened to me that when I was riding through the countryside, a loud whinnying would ring out from a stable where a pony

was kept singly as soon as our hoof beats approached. This pony was calling out to its fellow and would have liked to run with him, sniff him, and play with him. In a case like this we should not hesitate to speak to the owner. Maybe he would be delighted to have his pony go with us, with or without its rider, and this might be the beginning of a happy association. I would recommend to all keepers of single ponies that they get in touch with other pony people. Such contact can lead to sociable expeditions on horseback, to sharing pastures, or to mutual looking after each other's ponies during vacations.

Usually single ponies live in rural areas or on the periphery of cities where other ponies can generally be found. Spending some time together with another pony is a very welcome change in the life of a pony that is kept singly. Such a change is particularly important for stabled ponies who lack not only company but also sufficient exercise. If there are neither ponies nor horses to be found nearby, sharing a pasture with cattle or sheep (page 38) may be an acceptable alternative. If this is not feasible either, the pony has to be provided with adequate exercise by being ridden or lunged. If we spend a lot of time with the pony, or if children play with it, this also serves to break up the monotony of its life. But be careful not to pamper it and especially not to overfeed it (page 43). You want to make sure it keeps its native hardiness.

Foals must never grow up alone if they are to develop normally. They belong together with other foals as soon as they are weaned. Playing, racing around, nipping, tussling—in short, horseplay—is part of their natural development.

Care and Grooming

Keeping a Pony in a Stable

Most ponies used for riding and driving spend their lives in some kind of a stable, whether it be an open barn or a stall. If a pony is kept in a stall, it has to be tied very short so that it will not get entangled in the rope. It is therefore worse off than a chained dog (animal lovers are at work trying to improve these poor beasts' lot). If every single owner of a pony were to reject the stall for his pony, this cruelty to animals would soon be a thing of the past.

Cleanliness, Order—Light and Air

Whether you keep your pony in an open barn or stall, it must be:
• Airy, dry, and bright. This means that doors and windows have to be opened regularly. Do not allow humid warmth to develop; it promotes disease agents and lowers the pony's resistance.
• Made injury-proof. This means no splinters or sharp edges in the walls; no nails or hooks (nails can work their way out of wood in the course of wear, as when the pony pushes against a wooden wall); no exposed wires within the pony's reach (an electric shock is usually fatal for a pony).
• Clean and neat. Remove manure and clean the aisle and yard daily (do not leave the wheelbarrow full of manure in the stable). Keeping everything neat and clean makes the work easier and saves time and annoyance. It takes just a few minutes to clean off tools (manure fork, broom, pail, and wheelbarrow) and put them away where they belong. Trying to find these items when you have forgotten just where you left them and scraping off the caked dirt is much more time consuming. The whole stable and everything in it has to be scrubbed periodically and sometimes disinfected (mandatory after an illness, after worm infestations, and in the summer when ponies are plagued by flies and mosquitoes).

Bedding

Bedding is very important to the health and comfort of the pony. It should be dry, warm, soft, and as dust-free as possible. There are three common kinds of bedding for the floor of the barn.
• Loose straw that is changed several times a week or preferably every day. Straw makes a warm, clean bedding that feels good to the pony and is good for its hoofs. Straw, of course, must be dry. However, straw is not a good choice for ponies that start eating it either out of gluttony or boredom. This gives them big "straw bellies" and wrecks your feeding plan. A general disadvantage of straw is that it contains dust, which can irritate the pony's respiratory system. Being smaller than a regular horse, a pony is closer to the source of dust and therefore more likely to be bothered by it.
• Peat or wood shavings. With this kind of bedding, droppings should be removed promptly, and wet areas dug up and the holes filled in with fresh peat or shavings. Then the bedding should be loosened with the manure fork and afterward smoothed again evenly. This kind of bedding is warm, soft, acts as a deodorant, and is relatively dust-free. It is suitable for ponies that are allergic to dust or have respiratory problems (see Heaves, page 52) as well as for gluttonous ponies.
• Mattress bedding. This should more properly be called a permanent sub-bedding. It consists of a layer of well-packed peat or wood shavings that is covered with plenty of straw. Droppings and wet straw should be removed promptly. The packed straw is left in place, and fresh straw added whenever needed. In this way the mattress is built up. Do not try to "turn" the mattress because the

Care and Grooming

lower layers, at various stages of bacterial decomposition, give off a strong and unpleasant odor (ammonia fumes) that the pony is exposed to when it lies down. Remove the entire mattress one to four times a year, disinfect the floor, and build a new mattress.

If you own your barn, you should decide in favor of loose straw or peat or wood shavings. Ponies are clean by nature, and they will reward our meticulous care by staying healthy and having a cheerful and even disposition.

A Boarding Stable

If you board your pony, you usually have little say in his care and feeding. If you are not satisfied with the way things are done, you can—this is acceptable in many boarding stables—take over the care of your pony yourself. This requires a considerable commitment of time and work, but it will make possible the kind of contact with your little friend that is really needed. In any case, you should ascertain that all the conditions for the pony's well-being (feed, care, bedding, and—where indicated—freedom of movement) are present *before* you board it. For many who live in the city and have little time to ride and spend with the pony, a boarding stable is the best solution available. Care, grooming, and feeding of the pony—also during vacation time—and regular visits by the veterinarian and the blacksmith can be provided there. The opportunity to use the indoor arena and outdoor trails at given hours is another advantage, particularly for riders who wish to compete. All agreements, cost of boarding, and other costs and fees are set down in a written contract. A liability insurance policy (page 8) may be required.

Exercise

Whatever form of stabling you choose—or are forced to settle for if your first desire proves unrealizable—you must make sure that your pony gets exercise. Some riders think "granting" their well-fed pony one hour a day in the ring will do. What is more, they expect their pony to perform right off during this one hour, forgetting about the other twenty-three hours of the day that their little comrade spends locked up in a tiny space. Exercise for the pony is not synonymous with carrying its master with saddle and bridle around the arena; it should also include times when the pony can romp around at will and without constraints. In many riding schools there are stated times when the horses and ponies are allowed loose in the indoor arena or outside ring or when they are at least allowed to run on the longe. You should make use of every opportunity to ride, even in bad weather. Other welcome changes are trail rides or vacations the pony spends on the pasture of a farm. Many farmers like to take in ponies like this for a small fee.

That ponies can grow very attached to their "homes" was made clear to me one day when we put a pony that was used to living in a barn out to pasture. To be sure, it was by itself. After a short while, it broke out of the pasture and, to my surprise, did not make for the freedom of the surrounding meadows and fields, but galloped straight back, tail flying high, to the barn, marched happily down the aisle, greeted its stablemates with a loud whinny, and stood still expectantly outside its stall. It was, of course, not just love for the stall and the feeding trough that brought the little runaway back from the luscious green pasture; it was also the presence of its fellows that it sought. A well-tended stable can be a happy place for a pony if it is given enough exercise.

Care and Grooming

Keeping a Pony Outdoors

It used to be considered inconceivable—and has been until quite recently—that ponies or horses be kept on an open pasture with just a shelter for protection during the winter cold and snow. They had to have a warm, closed barn. Anything else was sheer cruelty to animals. Today we know that horses and ponies need a mode of life that is in keeping with their nature and that exposure to the changing weather of the different seasons benefits their overall health. They are extremely adaptable, withstand the severe cold by growing a winter coat, and protect themselves against the heat by sweating. Awareness of this fact, which is being accepted only slowly, began to develop only after indigenous ponies from the cold northern zones—from Iceland and Norway and also from Great Britain and Ireland—were introduced into warmer climates. These ponies' way of life (being outdoors all year round) is in keeping with their sturdy build and the consistency of their coat with its dense, fatty undercoat and long, water-resistant cover hair. In the case of other, less robust pony breeds, the outdoors regimen, or primitive regimen as it is sometimes called, has to be modified to take into account specific conditions of climate and terrain.

The outdoors regimen requires an open shelter with a paddock and a pasture. As compensation for the loss of wide-open nature, the ponies are at least given a small plot of land where they can act out their need for running, moving freely, rolling, and playing. They are in the fresh air and feel the sun, rain, and wind. The shelter serves as a substitute for big, shady trees, hedges, and hollows found in nature. But, as any novice pony keeper will note with amazement, the ponies will not spend much time in the shelter. They are happiest out in the open. When they graze, they feed, as in the wild, in their natural rhythm, munching small amounts while moving about slowly. This is appropriate for their digestive system because ponies have very small stomachs.

One of the most crucial factors in providing ponies with as natural a life as possible is the company of others of their kind. This is true for all breeds. There should always be several ponies living together, with an absolute minimum of two. In cases of incompatibility, when ponies bite or kick each other, the combative antagonists have to be separated. Close off one or more pastures or partition off parts of the paddock or open shelter. Moving individual ponies around repeatedly often has a calming effect but requires close observation at the beginning.

Keeping the pasture in good condition (page 38) is important, and, depending on the season and the size and yield of the pasture, additional feed will have to be provided (hay, root vegetables, grain). Fresh water has to be available every day, too. Natural sources of water such as brooks are unfortunately rare. If there is a water line to the pasture, automatic waterers, fountains with water pumps, or drinking troughs can be set up. If there is no source of water on the land, a mobile water tank can be rigged up with some kind of water dispenser.

When all this is seen to, the ponies will thrive both physically and psychologically and develop all their powers. If they are not especially delicate and you do not object to their growing a thick winter coat, they can be kept outdoors year round. But they will have to do without the pasture during heavy rains or during the winter months when it has to be blocked off and protected from wear.

For the owner, keeping his pony outdoors offers a number of advantages. He can provide a healthy, natural life for his ponies with

Care and Grooming

relatively little work and at a cost considerably lower than that of boarding ponies. He does not have to exercise the ponies every day. This does not mean, of course, that he can just let them fend for themselves. There is always something that needs to be done, even during the seasons when the pasture offers all the necessary food. It is precisely during those times that some ponies gorge themselves into sleek roundness on the luscious and nutritious May grass and need to be brought into the paddock so that they will not grow obese or founder. Ponies do not need a lot of food, and they do not need to spend all day in the pasture in the months from May to August. Grazing for two or three hours in the morning and two hours in the evening provides them with plenty of food. The waterers should be checked daily and cleaned when necessary. In the winter you have to make sure that water pipes do not freeze and that thick ice does not form on standing water. Fences have to be checked. If you find mouse or—worse—rat droppings in the feed room, you have to combat these rodents because they cause quite a bit of damage, and rats can be carriers of rabies. Keeping cats is the best method to keep rodents away. If you cannot keep a cat, use traps or rodent poisons but exercise great care and follow all directions. Make sure children and pets are safe from them.

The open shelter has to be cleaned out every day, and the droppings have to be removed from the sandy ground of the paddock. Because of the danger of worm infestations (page 49), the manure has to be collected from the pasture several times a week, too. In many places, farmers will happily take away the horse manure. If not, it can be composted. In the latter case you have to make sure that enough heat develops in the compost heap and that it gets turned often enough for all the worm eggs and larvae to be killed.

The Pasture

Fencing That Is Secure and Appropriate

It is important to fence pastures (and paddocks) securely because ponies that get out not only endanger themselves but can also cause serious traffic accidents. All gates must also be locked tightly (a chain with a lock works best) because it happens not infrequently that passers-by and children will enter the pasture to pet the ponies and then fail to close the gate properly behind them. Another bad habit people indulge in with the best (but ill-guided) of intentions is feeding ponies. This can be very detrimental to the pony, but there is little you can do about it apart from putting up a sign saying "Please Do Not Feed."

There are all kinds of fences made of all kinds of materials with all kinds of price tags. The most attractive and the safest, as well as

Fences around pastures must be solid and easily visible for ponies. There are two choices: a rail fence, which is very durable, and . . .

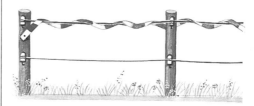

. . . a fence of plain or electric wire. For safety's sake this kind of fence should be marked with a strip of bright plastic.

Care and Grooming

the most expensive, solution is a wooden rail fence about 4½ feet (130 to 140 cm) high. If the wood is treated with a non-poisonous wood preservative, the fence will stand up a long time, and the ponies will not nibble on it. Since the pony has to be able to see the fence that marks the border of its territory, simple wires stretched between posts or electric fences are not suitable unless the wires are marked with colored plastic strips wrapped around them. This is still not an ideal solution, because part of the plastic will get lost in time and the fence becomes "invisible" again. It is better to string a plain wire or electric wire along the middle of the posts and use a special rubber or vinyl strip as the top strand. This is very durable and safe from biting. Never use barbed wire! Ponies cannot see it well and are very likely to get hurt on it. (Barbed-wire injuries can be very serious. The fence has to be checked periodically for rotting posts and torn wires. Ponies are very quick at spotting escapes.

Taking Care of the Pasture

You have to figure on at least 1 to 1½ acres of land for a small to medium-size pony. For larger ones you have to allow more. The wear on the pasture through the hoofs—whether shod or not—and through grazing is heavy. Horses and ponies nip off the grass with their lips and sharp incisors very close to the ground so that the crown of the plant often suffers. They also seek out their favorite herbs and leave the less tasty plants untouched. This leaves big tufts in the pasture that have to be mowed. To encourage more even grazing of the whole area you can, during the period of lush growth, subdivide the pasture into smaller plots with an easily movable electric fence (4 feet [1.2 m] high). The enclosed piece of pasture should be made into as long a rectangle as possible to give the pony enough room to gallop. Water has to be available on it. Meanwhile, the grass on the plots that are closed to grazing has a chance to grow, and in May and June parts of the pasture can be hayed. During long rainy spells even moving the ponies around from one part of the pasture to the other will not prevent damage to the turf. The ponies' sharp hoofs quickly penetrate through to the softened earth, and they must never be allowed to stand in the mud because this is very bad for their hoofs and legs. They therefore have to stay in the sandy paddock until the pasture dries out.

The proper care of a pasture involves not only collecting the ponies' droppings twice a week but also fertilizing the land. As a rule, pastures for horses and ponies should be fertilized only moderately, but the frequency with which the soil should be replenished and the kind and amount of fertilizer to be used depend on the kind of soil and the amount of wear. It is therefore hard to come up with specific prescriptions. Ask local farmers or your county extension agent for advice. I have had good results with organic fertilizers and lime. Any pasture that is used exclusively by ponies or horses or a combination of the two will gradually wear out and "tire of horses," and parasites will increase from year to year despite all your efforts at hygiene. One way to counter this situation is to pasture ponies together with sheep or cattle.

Pasturing with Horses, Cattle, or Sheep

If ponies are pastured together with horses, this does nothing to improve the pasture—on the contrary, the wear becomes heavier—but ponies like being with their big cousins. There may, of course, be cases of real antipathy. Petisa—to whom I keep coming back because she was the most independent-minded of all our ponies — shared a pasture for a while with our two big horses. She loved the company of the two geldings and kept wanting to play with them and tease them. The three were always near each other. One day, thinking she would be perfectly content there, we took her to another pasture where friends of ours kept their horses. She approached the horses, flattened her ears, turned, kicked, set off at a gallop, cleared the fence with an elegant leap, and left us and the startled horses standing there staring after her. On subsequent occasions she made friends with horses without the slightest problem, as is customary between horses and ponies.

Keeping ponies and cattle together on a pasture is very beneficial. The land is grazed more evenly, the grass improves in quality (partially because of the cow manure), and the danger of parasitic infestations is less. It was on a stud farm that I first learned how a herd of beef cattle—Aberdeen Angus in this particular case—can be used to free a large pasture of parasites by grazing it clean. Cattle, as well as sheep, eat the eggs and larvae of horse parasites along with the grass, and these parasites are destroyed in the process of digestion.

In the case of small pastures, sheep are often combined with ponies. With their different gait and way of biting off grass, they even out the growth in the pasture. In addition, sheep manure helps fertilize the grass. In contrast to their behavior toward horses, ponies react with indifference to sheep and cattle. There may be exceptions to this rule if there is only one of each kind of animal. We once kept a pony mare on a pasture with a ram whose ewe had been stolen. The pony mare and the ram made friends and became inseparable. One day I went with my small daughter to fetch the pony. I had taken the docile pony by the halter and led it a few steps when I heard a scream behind me. The ram had attacked the child, knocked her over with his horns, and was ready to charge again. If the farmer had not been close enough to interfere and drag the ram away with all his strength, the result could have been disastrous. I had learned my lesson. The jealous ram was supplied with a new ewe, and our pony was returned to the horse and pony pasture.

Caring for Your Pony

I have always enjoyed grooming a pony. You are close to your little friend; you talk to him, sing a song, or whistle. The pony in turn is happy to hear the familiar voice and have the pleasant sensation of being freed from dust, itchy sweat, and clumps of dirt. Brushing and currying are done not just for the sake of cleanliness. They are a kind of massage that stimulates the circulation and allows the skin to breathe, thus enhancing the pony's entire well-being. There is, however, a real difference in the grooming of a stabled pony and one that is pastured. The latter needs much less intense grooming. Rain, sun, and wind take care of some of the job, and if the pony can roll in the grass, snow, or dry sand and then shake itself vigorously, this also benefits the coat. If the pony rolls in the mud and its hair gets all caked, this is a different story. Then it has to be thoroughly cleaned, just as it should be before and after it is taken out for riding or pulling.

For cleaning you will need a body brush, a currycomb, a scrub brush, two sponges, an absorbent cloth, a mane comb, a hoof pick, and a hoof brush. Coarse dirt is brushed out. The currycomb should be used only sparingly on ponies that live outdoors. The winter coat should be left alone so that its waterproof and insulating qualities stay intact. But in the

Care and Grooming

spring, when the thick winter fur is shed, there is a need for vigorous brushing and currying. This is hard work for us, but it provides welcome relief to the pony. It goes without saying that the brushed-out hair has to be picked up right away, that ponies should never be cleaned in their pasture, paddock, or stall, and that they should be tied while they are being cleaned. You need to have a place for grooming where the pony does not otherwise spend time and, above all, where it does not eat. Stabled ponies, especially those used for sport, should be cleaned thoroughly every day. Anyone who has ever used a body brush and currycomb knows what enormous amounts of dust get absorbed in a pony's coat in no time at all. A barn apron, cap or kerchief, old gloves, and hard-soled shoes are recommended apparel for cleaning. The "cleaning hand" holds the body brush, the other hand the currycomb. You brush from front to back with long, vigorous strokes, starting at the neck. After each stroke, the brush has to be cleaned with the currycomb

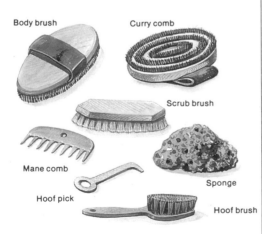

Body brush

Curry comb

Scrub brush

Mane comb

Hoof pick

Sponge

Hoof brush

The most important items needed for grooming a pony.

(toward the finger tips). As a general rule you brush with the lie of the hair, going against it only in very dirty spots. The currycomb is used on the pony only if the fur is caked with dirt. It is never used on the head, the legs, or any bony places.

The head has to be brushed very gently, and the eyes and nostrils cleaned cautiously with a sponge. Never cut the long hairs near the eyes, muzzle, and nostrils. Brush the mane well. If the use of a comb is necessary, do not pull or yank. The hair of the tail is combed through with your fingers; then it is brushed and, like the mane, washed occasionally. If it is very dirty, use hard soap. The hair at the fetlock is brushed but, if at all possible, should not be cut. All the hairless parts of the body are washed with the second sponge. Finally, the coat is rubbed with a cloth until it is smooth and glossy.

After Riding or Working

Any pony, whether stabled or pastured, must be properly cared for after working. If it is sweaty—especially under the saddle—it can be washed off with a sponge or, more commonly, rubbed dry with handfuls of straw or a towel. In warm weather the pony can be hosed down gently with a weak jet of water. Start with the legs, then move to the stomach, between the legs, and on to the back and croup. This feels very good to the pony. Afterward it has to be walked around or left in the sun until it is dry.

Care and Shoeing of the Hoofs

The expression "no feet, no horse" dramatically states the importance of the hoofs for ponies and horses. In contrast to people and many animals, such as dogs, horses spend little time lying down. They need not only sound legs and joints but also healthy hoofs to do the amount of standing, walking, trotting,

Care and Grooming

galloping, and jumping that is required of them. Keeping their hoofs sound is therefore an especially important part of grooming. Each step means a shock of heavy weight that has to be absorbed. The hoof is the lowest digit on the horse's foot. A complex structure that has to be both elastic and solid, it consists of the coffin bone, the soft inner parts (laminae), and the surrounding horny shell made up of the horny wall, the sole, and the triangular frog with its central cleft. The horny parts have no nerve endings and are therefore not sensitive to pain, but they can be injured (the frog less than the sole). Between the lower rim of the horny wall, the carrying edge, and the sole, there is the white line into which the nails are driven when the horse is shod. The daily care of the hoofs consists of picking them out in the morning. The cleaning before and after any outing or job should be especially thorough. Foreign bodies that are lodged or stuck in the foot are carefully removed. The hoofs are washed inside and outside (only brushed and wiped with a damp cloth if it is cold) and then lightly painted with fresh hoof dressing or baby oil, especially at the coronet where the horn terminates in skin. Painting prevents the horny parts of the hoof from getting brittle and splitting.

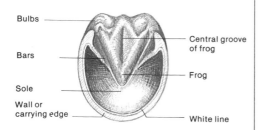

Bulbs
Bars
Sole
Wall or carrying edge
Central groove of frog
Frog
White line

This is what the underside of a hoof looks like. Hoofs need special care.

The hoof care of ponies that live on a pasture that is in good shape does not have to be so elaborate. Still, the hoofs have to be checked regularly and cared for as needed. Whether a pony should be "barefoot"—which strengthens its hoofs—or shod depends on how it is used and on what kind of ground it walks. Since the horny parts keep growing, the hoofs of unshod ponies have to be trimmed and shaped every eight to twelve weeks. Many ponies are shod to protect the hoofs and keep the soles from getting too worn. Depending on how the pony is used and how fast the hoof wall grows, a pony has to be shod every six to eight weeks unless a shoe comes loose or falls off earlier. The hind feet and front feet and the right and left feet are all differently shaped. The shoes have to be fitted precisely to the trimmed hoofs. The iron has to match the carrying edge of the foot exactly and without leaving any cracks between shoe and hoof. The proper shoeing of a horse is an art. Incorrect fit can damage joints, bring about lameness, and cause cracks and injuries to the coronet. Incorrectly set nails can enter the laminae (page 48), causing the pony pain and laming it. But most disorders of the hoofs are due to humid floors, moist and moldy bedding, overworking of the pony, and incorrect feeding. Problems of the hoofs are dangerous and difficult to clear up. Conscientious care of the hoofs and appropriate shoeing are therefore of top priority in keeping a pony.

Breeding—the Pros and Cons

Planned breeding is a necessity in domestic animals because it duplicates what nature does with wild animals, namely, ensuring the survival of the fittest. Breeding in the literal sense means the planned increase—the producing and raising—of animals, but in the larger sense it involves knowledge, experience, responsibility, and tradition. That is why only accomplished breeders should engage in this activity. They know how arduous the path is that leads to success. What we need are high-quality ponies that embody the ideal of their breed and sex and that are suitable for the intended use. Breeding associations and reputable private breeders see to it that the breeding stock is properly chosen. Stallions have to be officially selected for stud service, and brood mares have to be listed in official registers.

Understandable as it is that owners of ponies, especially children, wish for a foal, random breeding or, more accurately, thoughtless increase is undesirable. The resulting ponies will be of some indeterminate type, and in most cases conditions are not conducive to a healthy pregnancy for the mare or, later, to the raising of the foal. Foals have to grow up playing and horsing around with other young foals in a pasture to develop normally. Then, too, people easily forget that the precious and cute little baby foal will soon turn into a strong young pony that is not so easy to keep and that will be ready for training and use only years later. Another thing to remember is that your much desired foal will live for about twenty years and that somebody will have to take care of it this whole time. These are the reasons why many of these animals are then offered for sale. But because of the large supply of ponies available today, buyers may be hard to find, and these animals are therefore often given away free to whoever will take them. Few people realize how many of them end up in the slaughterhouse. Love for animals, common sense, and a sense of responsibility all point to the same thing: planned breeding—yes; indiscriminate breeding—no.

Proper Nutrition

Ponies are light and undemanding eaters. Their basic food is hay and grass. They should get grain; for example, oats, only after special exertion as when they have been used for sports, for demanding trail riding, or after they have been made to pull carriages or buggies. We should go light on food with ponies that are not worked hard because their appetite is always good. Being overfed (page 47) interferes with the performance of the pony and can make it sick. It is impossible to list specific amounts of food that are appropriate for all ponies because each individual utilizes food differently, and the work it does affects its needs. Also, food varies in nutritional value. All I can give you are some guidelines; every keeper of ponies will have to determine the exact amounts and composition himself on the basis of experience and observation (you should be able to feel the ribs of the pony but not see them).

General Rules

• In the spring and summer, pastured ponies should be allowed to graze only a few hours a day. Mornings and evenings are best (there are fewer flies). Wait in the morning until the dew has evaporated; otherwise there is a danger of absorbing worm larvae (page 49). Feed hay in the late fall and winter.
• Any change in feed — from pasture to hay and vice versa — has to be gradual. The same is true for ponies kept in stables.
• The feed must be of excellent quality to prevent intestinal problems, colic, and other diseases. Hay must not be musty, dusty, or moldy (this can cause heaves, page 52). Oats that have germinated are unusable. Hay and oats have to be seasoned, and green fodder should not be fed still warm from the sun or wilted.

• Food and water containers must be kept clean. Leftover food ferments easily, and this can give rise to colic.
• Give food punctually at regular intervals.
• Feed several times a day, preferably in the morning, at noon, and in the evening. The relatively small stomach of a pony cannot absorb a lot of food at once. If possible, do not feed right before work. The main meal should be in the evening when the pony will have time to digest.
• Never place the hay on the floor but instead in as wide a rack as possible.
• The pony must have peace while it eats; do not disturb it while it eats by cleaning it, removing its bedding, or saddling it.
• The pony always has to have fresh water that is clean and free of odor. Ponies need a lot of water. If there is no automatic waterer, water has to be provided three or four times a day, preferably before feedings.
• If the pony is overheated, it must not be allowed to drink until cool.

Kinds of Food

Green Fodder
This consists of regular grass (pasture), clover, and young fodder oats. All these have to be very fresh.

Roughage
This consists of hay and straw (also chopped) as well as bedding straw. Green fodder and roughage form the basis of a pony's nutrition.

Succulent Foods
Turnips, carrots, apples, and potatoes belong in this category. These are usually given as treats or rewards as an addition to the

Right: At pony shows and events the performances of both ▷
the pony and the rider are judged. Above, jumping;
below, running walk.

basic food. The tops of carrots and potatoes that have sprouted must not be fed. They can cause colic.

High-Energy Food

These usually consist of grain, especially oats. Grain can be stretched and made more easily digestible by the addition of chopped straw or bran. When Petisa could not be pastured, we used to feed her oats mixed with moistened bran, as we did our horses, but in smaller amounts.

Commercial Feeds

Commercial feed—usually in the form of pellets—is made up of all the different necessary foods and is a concentrated food. It may be a supplemental mixture of oats, wheat bran, molasses, linseed, soy meal, dehydrated grass meal, vitamins, and minerals meant to be given in addition to hay. It is dust-free. Other compositions that include the above elements with an addition of dehydrated alfalfa meal as roughage are also ready to use. They are fed without additional hay or straw and are therefore not very suitable for ponies except for competition ponies.

Mash

This provides an excellent special diet to be fed after great exertion, after contests and hunts, when the pony is weak after an illness, and after shedding. This nutritious supplemental food consists of rolled oats, wheat bran, and linseed. Pour boiling water over it, mix, and offer twice a week in the evening. In cases of lack of appetite add a little molasses.

Food Supplements

Since a pony's basic foods often are low in vitamins and trace elements, these can be given in the form of powders or pellets as a supplement to hay and oats. Vitamins can also be prescribed by a veterinarian. To make up for the lack of minerals in the basic foods, a salt lick (with or without iodine and copper) should be placed in the barn and the pasture.

Poisonous Plants

Instinct and a fine sense of smell usually keep ponies from getting poisoned by eating the wrong plants. But if a pony has been overtaxed or is tired and weak, these natural guardians may fail, and the consequences may be disastrous. Just a few branches (6 or 7 ounces [200 g]!) of the evergreen yew, which is often planted in gardens and parks, can be fatal for a pony. Ponies usually avoid poisonous plants on the pasture, and most of these plants are no longer harmful when they are dry; that is, in the hay. Some exceptions are: spring adonis, autumn crocus, horsetail, and bracken fern.

Some *extremely poisonous* plants are boxwood, jimson weed, and deadly nightshade. Other poisonous plants are black locust, golden chain, ligustrum, strawberry bush, spurge laurel, juniper, poison hemlock, horsetail, buttercup, foxglove, tobacco, narcissus, hyacinth, and lily-of-the-valley.

If you are not familiar with these plants, look them up and read the descriptions in a guide to poisonous plants.

Keeping Your Pony Healthy

◁ Left: New Forest pony

Because of their general resilience and healthy constitution, ponies are less subject to disease than full-size horses. This does not mean, however, that ponies never get sick. They are just as likely to be injured as horses. Thus, any pony owner should know how to keep a pony healthy and deal with possible illnesses. Apart from regular vaccinations, deworming, and absolute cleanliness in stable and pasture, the most important requirement is to keep your pony in a manner that is consistent with its natural hardiness. Coddled and overfed ponies that are confined to warm and humid quarters quickly lose their resistance to adverse weather and carriers of disease. They are more prone to disorders like founder, and when they are affected with diseases that keep them from eating they can die of hyperlipemia. A healthy pony is lively and cheerful, moves freely, has a good appetite, bright eyes, and a natural sheen or gloss to its coat.

The pulse, breathing, and temperature should be normal when the pony has not been exercising.
• Pulse: 30 to 44 (in foals, up to 60) regular beats per minutes. Check by placing your middle and index fingers in the depression under the lower jaw.
• Breathing: 10 to 16 regular breaths per minute. Watch the rising of the rib cage.
• Temperature: 99.5 to 100.8°F (37.5 to 38.2°C); in foals, 99.5 to 101.3°F (37.5 to 38.5°C); in newborn foals, up to 102.2°F (39°C). The temperature is taken rectally. Attach a string to the thermometer to prevent it from falling to the ground or slipping down into the intestine. Lubricate the tip with oil or Vaseline. To prevent being kicked when inserting the thermometer, stand on the left of the pony near the croup and raise the root of the tail; if the animal is nervous, have someone lift up its left foreleg.

Any change in the general state of health can signal the onset of a disease that should be diagnosed and treated as early as possible. The pony should then be subjected to close observation, preferably in a clean, draft-free stall with plenty of fresh, dry bedding, and be kept as quiet and isolated as possible. Enter the first change you observe and the symptoms in your pony journal. These records will provide useful background for future occasions and may prove useful for the veterinarian who has to be consulted for most illnesses. You should have some basic knowledge about injuries and illnesses and how to treat and cure them. Above all, you must be familiar with the principles of first aid in order to react correctly in an emergency before the veterinarian arrives.

A Medicine Chest for the Stable

No stable should be without a first-aid kit to handle emergencies and routine procedures. The contents of a well-stocked first-aid kit should include: absorbent cotton, soap or detergent, veterinary thermometer with thong, gauze squares, blunt scissors, alcohol, a roll of adhesive tape, antimicrobial ointment, cleansing antiseptic (such as hydrogen peroxide), body wash or liniment, and bandages.

Wounds and Their Treatment

In the course of a lifetime a pony almost inevitably sustains some minor and sometimes major injuries. These usually require immediate action, and the pony owner has to be prepared to render first aid. At these times it is terribly important to know if and when the wounded pony was vaccinated against tetanus (check in your pony journal). Annual tetanus shots should be administered as a matter of

Keeping Your Pony Healthy

course. If the pony has not had these shots, a preventive treatment with serum and antibiotics should be initiated immediately by a veterinarian. In the case of vaccinated animals, especially when there are deep puncture wounds, antibiotics and a booster tetanus shot are advisable.

Minor injuries or surface wounds generally heal easily and quickly. They should be disinfected immediately with soap or a cleansing antiseptic and treated with sulfonamide or antibiotic powder. Make sure the wound stays absolutely clean, especially in the summer when the danger of flies depositing their eggs in the wound is greatest. In the case of major injuries or deep wounds, remain calm, try to prevent excessive loss of blood, and call the veterinarian, who will usually have to sew up the wound. Keep the pony in a quiet and dust-free spot and do not apply any disinfectants before the veterinarian arrives. If you use a disinfectant, this may make it impossible to sew up the wound. You should also refrain from washing or probing the wound because you may introduce dirt and increase the danger of infection in the process.

Arterial bleeding (bright red blood issuing from the wound in a regular rhythm) can be controlled until the arrival of the vet by squeezing the artery between two fingers (use sterile gauze). Bleeding can also be stilled by applying cotton or a sterile gauze square or by applying a tight bandage: Lay some sterile gauze and then a layer of cotton or other absorbent material on the wound and squeeze tightly against it with a bandage. In the case of a large wound on the body, use a flat object (a book or large wooden plate) to help you press. If the bleeding is very heavy, the wound has to be tied off: Apply a tourniquet (improvised, if on an outing, with a strip of cloth and a stick) above the wound; that is, between the wound and the heart. The tourni-

quet should not stay on for more than a half hour. Then it should be taken off for a minute to allow the blood to get to the tissue; afterward, it should be put back on a little below where it was located before. Continue like this until the veterinarian arrives.

Injuries near the eyes should be treated with boric acid solution. Never use strong disinfectants.

Fresh bruises should be cooled by running cold water over them or applying frequently changed cold compresses. Afterward, massage with liniment or soak with warm water and Epsom salts.

Foreign objects embedded in the hoof (e.g., nails) have to be slowly and carefully pulled out at the same angle at which they entered. Check to make sure that the whole object is removed. Then disinfect the wound and have it treated by the veterinarian. Keep the pony quiet in its stall for a few days. Injuries caused by incorrectly placed nails in the horseshoe also have to be treated by the veterinarian.

If the pony has saddle sores, it is absolutely essential that these be taken care of. Disinfect the sores and apply cold poultices of a white lotion or sulfonamide powder. These sores clear up slowly. Make sure to remedy the cause by fixing the part of the saddle or saddle blanket that has been rubbing.

Controlling Parasites

Parasites, which plague a pony and endanger its health, are the main curse in a pony's life. That is why regular preventive checks and worm cures are necessary. External parasites—lice, mites (which lead to mange)—are relatively rare, easy to recognize, and can be effectively combatted. Lice (in the long hair) or mites (especially in the fetlocks) may be a sign of inadequate cleanliness or care. Treat

Keeping Your Pony Healthy

with benzene hexachloride or wash with a medicated soap.

The various kinds of internal parasites are much more dangerous, and their presence is harder to determine. They may have attacked and weakened the pony before they can be spotted in the feces. Foals should be treated for threadworms (*Strongyloides*) during their first week, and they should be wormed thereafter every two or three months. Depending on how infested the pasture or stable is (have feces analyzed to check on this), a grown pony should be wormed two to four times a year. The absolute minimum is once in the spring. If possible, the pony should be moved to a parasite-free pasture at the same time. If a pasture is heavily infested with parasites, changing the grazing population to ruminants or haying the field helps. A record should be kept of the wormings, and the veterinarian should be consulted as to what the most effective medication is. The insidious thing about internal parasites is that they go through their cycle from worm to egg to larva and back to worm while passing from host animal to feces to stable floor or pasture to feed and back to

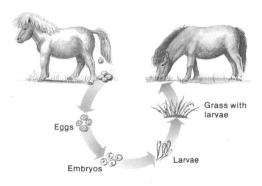

Eggs

Embryos

Larvae

Grass with larvae

The vicious cycle of parasitic infestation with blood worms.

host, thus constantly reinfecting the animal. In contrast to wild ponies, our stabled or pastured ones have to seek their food near their droppings. This gives rise to a vicious cycle of reinfection and causes the spreading of the parasites.

Blood worms (*strongyles*) are among the most common intestinal parasites. These bloodsucking worms, varying in length from ¼ to 1 ¼ inches (.5 to 3.5 cm), afflict almost all ponies and horses, including foals, and can be deadly if present in large masses. The larvae are picked up in the feed—hay, straw, or wet grass—and then pass through a slow development (up to eleven months) in various organs and the bloodstream of the host. The damage is considerable and continues when the sexually mature worms attach themselves to the intestines. Their eggs are excreted in the feces and develop, if there is enough moisture, into new larvae. The whole cycle then starts all over again unless they are effectively combatted.

Roundworms (*ascarids*) also attack horses and ponies while they are still foals and can reach epidemic proportions. They feed on the contents of the small intestine, excreting substances that harm the animal. The extremely resilient eggs of the roundworms are passed in the feces of the pony and, by way of the feed, end up again in the pony's small intestine. Here they evolve into larvae that burrow through the intestinal wall and develop to sexual maturity while wandering through the bloodstream and the lungs. Damage to internal organs, emaciation, anemia, diarrhea, and abnormal development of the foal can result from roundworm infestations. The same is true for threadworms, which attack ponies in particular.

If a pony rubs its rump a lot against any and all available objects, this is a sign that it has pinworms (*Oxyuris equi*), relatively harmless but annoying parasitic worms a little over ½ inch (1.5 cm) long. The adult worm deposits masses of eggs near the anal opening, where they cause intense itching. Cleaning around the anus with a special sponge and keeping the stable clean can prevent reinfection by eggs ingested in the food. In many cases the itching is caused by other reasons.

Luckily, tapeworms are quite rare in ponies and horses. These parasites are not destroyed by the normal worm medications, and if a pony suffers from lack of appetite, diarrhea, or emaciation, tapeworms may be the cause. The veterinarian has to administer treatment for this.

The common botfly or leg fly (*Gasterophilus*) is a parasite whose life cycle takes up a whole year. During the summer months it flies around, laying its easily visible, yellowish-white, oval eggs in the hair of the pony's forelegs. Grazing ponies are most exposed. As soon as the ponies lick their legs to relieve the itching, larvae, which have in the meantime developed inside the eggs, hatch in response to the moisture of the saliva. These larvae burrow into the tissue of the mouth and tongue and move to the stomach after three or four weeks, where they attach themselves to the stomach lining. They stay there ten to twelve months before they are passed out in the manure. After a pupa stage of three to five weeks, the new botfly hatches. Treatment should be administered in December and January when the botfly in all its stages is in the digestive tract and can be destroyed there.

Washing the legs several times with warm water and wine vinegar, carefully removing and destroying the deposited eggs, and treatment by the veterinarian help to get rid of the botfly. One effective method is to place the pony with its infected legs on heavy paper and scrape off the glued-on eggs with a safety razor without a blade in it. Burn the paper and the eggs immediately.

Illnesses and Their Treatment

Of the various diseases that can attack ponies, only a few will be mentioned and briefly discussed here. If any of these diseases occur, you will—unless years of experience qualify you to deal with the case at hand yourself—have to call the veterinarian. Nevertheless, any pony owner should be able to recognize the onset of a disease and interpret its symptoms correctly.

General Symptoms of Illness
A pony indicates that it is sick in various ways: lack of appetite, restlessness or apathy, breaking into a sweat, diarrhea, stiffness or lameness, dull eyes, discharge from the nose, dull, mussed hair, difficulty in breathing, coughing, and so on. At any of these signs, you should immediately check the pony's breathing, pulse, and temperature and keep it quiet in its stall, which must be dry and free of dust. If you are uncertain about what to do, you should call the veterinarian right away because improper treatment can quickly cause harm that even the vet cannot undo later.

Diseases for Which There Are Vaccines
Because it is so highly contagious and spreads so rapidly, influenza is one of the most feared diseases that affect horses and ponies. It is a virus disease accompanied by fever and occurs most frequently during the warm season. Foals and young ponies are especially prone to influenza. The symptoms are fever, a watery discharge from the nose, and a dry, racking cough. The pony needs absolute quiet, treatment by the veterinarian, and solicitous care. It has to be kept isolated

and may not be exercised until the condition is completely cleared up. There is a vaccine against influenza. The pony should have two initial innoculations at an interval of six weeks and then have yearly booster shots.

Tetanus shots should be given in the same pattern. Ponies and horses are very susceptible to tetanus or lockjaw, which can be caused by minute injuries (for example, barbed-wire scratches, stepping on a nail), and regular tetanus shots are therefore crucial. The incubation period for lockjaw is two days to six weeks, and the symptoms are stiff movements, difficulty in swallowing, and inability to get up (can be confused with colic). Call the veterinarian immediately!

The danger of rabies is not great for ponies, but since this disease is incurable in man and animals and is extremely painful in its terminal stage, ponies should—especially in areas where rabies is common—be vaccinated yearly against it. Possible signs of this disease are restlessness, difficulty in swallowing, paralysis, colic-like symptoms, and foaming at the mouth. If there is the slightest suspicion of rabies call the vet immediately.

Colic

This is painful intestinal disorder that can attack very suddenly may have different causes: unhealthy (spoiled) food, overheated green fodder, cold water (which overheated ponies drink up too fast), overexertion, colds, poisoning, worm infestation, or faulty teeth. Some typical symptoms are: restlessness, refusing to eat, pawing the ground, breaking into a sweat, frequent looking around at or trying to kick the stomach, repeated lying down, rolling, and inability to urinate and defecate. The veterinarian should be called immediately. Until he arrives the pony is not to be fed. You may give it lukewarm but not cold water. The pony should be walked, pref-

erably in a protected spot and with a rug for warmth. Try to prevent the pony from throwing itself on the ground and rolling. Gentle massaging of the belly and flanks with diluted brandy brings relief until the veterinarian arrives. Then follow the vet's directions conscientiously. Colic is the most frequent source of death in horses and consequently has to be taken very seriously.

Leg and Hoof Ailments

Here, as in everything else, an ounce of prevention is better than a pound of cure. The necessary precautionary measures are: Do not overwork the pony; give it sufficient and regular exercise, the right amount of healthy food, and plenty of dry bedding. Keep the stall meticulously clean; check the hoofs daily and have them shod by a blacksmith; allow plenty of pasture time. In addition, ponies that are used for showing or eventing may benefit from wearing exercise bandages or protective boots.

Founder is an inflammation of the laminae of the feet. This serious disorder of the hoofs usually occurs on the forelegs. Incorrect or overly rich food, long periods of standing, overexertion of the forelegs, and allergies are possible causes. The inflammation sets in very suddenly and is accompanied by very little fever but very high pulse. Other signs are standing with the forefeet extended forward, and heat, swelling, and the formation of characteristic rings as the laminae are destroyed. Keep the pony quiet and call the veterinarian because this disorder can become chronic and even lead to death.

Spavin is an ossification on the inner side of the hock. It can be the result of a sprain, an injury, or of overexertion. Absolute quiet and veterinary treatment are necessary. Spavin can lead to chronic lameness.

Swellings that are caused by an oversecretion of joint fluid are neither very dangerous nor painful and are therefore considered blemishes rather than a serious unsoundness. They can occur at the elbow, at the hock joint or just above it, or at the fetlocks.

Longitudinal cracking of the horn of the hoof starting either at the coronet or the carrying edge can, if treated promptly, be cured by the blacksmith with the proper kind of horseshoe. Deep cracks have to be treated by the veterinarian. To prevent cracks, take proper and regular care of the hoofs.

Thrush is a bacterial disease caused by inadequate hoof care, lack of cleanliness, and above all by wet and dirty bedding. Thrush turns the frog of the foot black and brittle, and a sticky, foul-smelling substance forms in the furrows. The treatment consists of immediate cleaning of the hoof and removal by the smith of the decaying portions of the horn. Disinfect the stable, replace bedding daily with fresh, dry litter, and look after the hoof (treat with wood tar only after fully healed).

Shoe boils are also caused by lack of cleanliness and excess moisture or improper food. Malanders are oozing sores at the elbow. Rest, thorough cleaning, use of mild disinfectants, applications of powder to keep the affected area dry, and diet feeding are effective measures.

Summer Eczema

Summer eczema is an allergic skin reaction (not contagious) that occurs from May to October. Icelandic ponies raised in their native country are particularly subject to this ailment. For years, fighting this disorder, which is especially annoying to the animal because of the intense itching it causes, was considered very difficult. Then it was discovered that the ailment is an allergic reaction to the stinging mosquitoes of the *Stomoxys* and *Colicoides* genera, and effective means to combat these

mosquitoes have been found. The mosquitoes are out only during the warm months and are active primarily in the hours preceding and following sunset. They bite mainly the skin at the top of the mane and near the withers, croup, and tail. Sometimes they also attack the neck, back, belly, and the base of the ears. Sensitive animals react with small swellings of the skin that can lead to pussy infections. Because of the itching, most ponies wear the hair off the affected places by rubbing. In the fall the allergy subsides. As a precautionary measure for ponies that react strongly to these mosquitoes, the stable should be treated during the summer with an appropriate insecticide to get rid of the mosquitoes. Pastured ponies should be brought inside for two hours before and after sunset—or entirely, if that is impossible—and fed high-energy feed and hay. Ponies that already show symptoms should have the affected places carefully cleaned and have medication, prescribed by the veterinarian, rubbed into the skin. In many cases, a treatment with a medicated oil helps.

Serious Diseases

Heaves is caused by chronic emphysema. The heart is also affected. The disease manifests itself in rapid, or "double," breathing and a chronic cough. The condition is incurable. It can be somewhat alleviated by using the pony for light work only, keeping him at pasture, and avoiding dust. Heaves and similar ailments are not uncommon among Icelandic ponies, which tend to be allergic.

Hydrocephalus is an incurable disease of the brain, usually caused by an accumulation of fluid in the brain. Alertness and sensitivity are severely affected, and the pony seems lethargic and disinterested.

Roaring is caused by a chronic disorder of the larynx or trachea. A paralysis of the vocal cords affects the breathing and causes a whistling sound. The condition is incurable.

Periodic ophthalmia, also called moonblindness, is an inflammation of the eye, which, if it goes unattended, leads to blindness. If the conjunctivas are swollen and red and the eyes are tearing, the veterinarian should be called promptly.

Glanders is a contagious, almost always fatal disease that has been virtually wiped out in the United States, thanks to a program of testing suspected cases and destroying confirmed cases.

Encephalomyelitis is an incurable disease caused by a virus that induces inflammation of the brain and spinal cord. The symptoms are fever, depression, walking in circles, wandering into obstacles, refusing to eat or drink, and sleepiness—all eventually resulting in paralysis and death. It is transmitted by mosquitoes and has three strains: Western (WEE), Eastern (EEE), and Venezuelan (VEE). The disease can be prevented by innoculation each spring.

Equine infectious anemia (swamp fever) is also an incurable disease carried by a virus. The EIA virus destroys the walls of blood vessels and causes massive destruction of red blood cells, resulting in depression, weakness, uncoordination, and a high fever of up to 106°. Often there is a period of recovery after an acute phase, then a relapse. There is no vaccine—only a test, called the Coggins Test, to determine if the animal has the disease. There is no cure, and affected animals should be destroyed to prevent infection of others.

Understanding Ponies

There is much useful information that can help us understand the nature and behavior of ponies.

Body Structure and External Characteristics

Anyone who owns a pony should be familiar with the basics of pony anatomy. This will make it clear how you can place your weight on the pony and how you can lighten its burden when riding, and you will understand the different motions involved in the various gaits and in jumping. Since the elbow and the knee of a pony or horse do not look like ours, people sometimes think that the hoof, which is really a toe, is the foot; the cannon, the calf; and the forearm, the thigh. The tarsi, or hocks, of the rear legs play a crucial function in all the pony's movements, as do the knees of the forelegs. The hocks and knees lend smoothness to the gaits and absorb the shock of the weight coming down on the ground, the knees absorbing the greatest part of the shock in jumping.

When dealing with ponies and horses we speak of forequarters and hindquarters. The forequarters take in the head, the neck, the withers, and the forelegs. The forequarters must not be overstrained by the rider's sitting too far forward (this is easy to do with ponies whose withers are generally not very pronounced). The croup and the hindlegs belong to the hindquarters. They provide the power and impetus for forward motion and jumping. The legs carry and hold up the body, and their joints are subject to strenuous wear. A

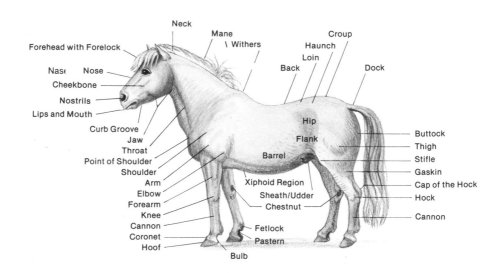

Pony anatomy. Shown here are the major parts of the body.

Vaulting is an excellent preparatory exercise for horseback ▷ riding. The Haflinger is especially well suited for this.

considerate rider will therefore not gallop across hard surfaces (asphalt) or excessively soft ground (sandy dunes, boggy moors). He will post lightly at a trot (easing the strain on the pony's back as well) and sit lightly when galloping fast or jumping.

For judging body structure and appearance, the standards for ponies vary slightly from those for horses in certain characteristics or "points." The configuration of the legs demanded in saddle horses is not required of ponies. On the contrary, unconventional leg posture (as in New Forest or Bosnian Mountain ponies) or toes pointing out (Icelandic pony) do not detract from the quality of the pony. Knock-knees, which are quite common in Dülmen, Welsh, Exmoor, Dartmoor, and Shetland ponies, are considered a sign of surefootedness.

Physical differences among breeds are so marked that a description of ponies can be given only in the most general terms. The head of a pony is supposed to be muscular, expressive, and not too heavy. The neck should be well muscled. A compact, square body and solid, stocky legs are further pony characteristics. The croup is steep in many breeds, and the tail sits low. The shape of the hoofs varies too. Mountain ponies have small, extremely hard hoofs. Ponies from areas where moors and bogs predominate have wider hoofs. One characteristic shared by many breeds is the low withers. For these ponies, the saddle should be equipped with a crupper to keep it secure in the proper position.

The Coat

The coat and the long hair (main, forelock, tail, fetlocks, and whiskers) of many pony breeds come in many variations of the basic

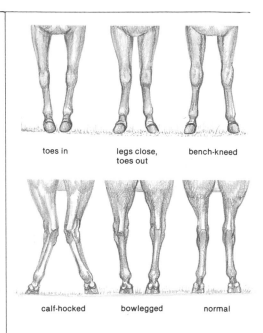

toes in   legs close, toes out   bench-kneed

calf-hocked   bowlegged   normal

Placement of the front legs (above) and hind legs (below).

colors. Icelandic ponies and Shetlands are cases in point. Some other breeds are fairly uniform in coloration. Haflingers are chestnut colored, Camargue ponies are almost always white, and Fjord ponies are dun.

The color of the mane and tail differs from the color of the coat in most ponies. The main colors are:
• Chestnut: light reddish brown, reddish brown, or dark reddish brown; long hair is light or reddish brown.
• Brown: light brown, brown, dark brown, or black brown; long hair is black.
• Black: all black to pitch black, including long hair.

Understanding Ponies

- White: white ponies are born with a dark coat that changes to white gradually over several years; long hair, white.
- Palomino: cream, yellow gray, or buff; long hair is light to whitish.
- Dun: almost white, yellow, or sand to darker shades; long hair, black; often with dorsal stripe.
- Pinto: large patches of color on a different ground color; black and brown, black and white (piebald), brown and white (skewbald), red and white.
- Appaloosa: white with many round spots of a different color.

In most pony breeds, the hair of the mane, tail, and forelock is long and thick. When properly looked after, this hair is not only beautiful but also serves as a good protection against flies. Leave it uncut if possible. One special feature of many ponies (as in Icelandic ponies) is a rain cover, an umbrella-like formation of hair about 4 inches (10 cm) long that fans out at the base of the tail. Rain and snow slide off this "umbrella," leaving the anus and, in the case of mares, the vagina dry when the pony turns its posterior into a storm, as ponies generally do. The fetlock hair, too, is functional: It sheds water and lessens the danger of injury or infection of the sensitive fetlock joint. It should not be cut either. Never remove the whiskers on lips and chin; they have an important function (page 59).

Patches of white hair on the head and the feet constitute the individual markings of a pony. Stars or blazes, white lips, white fetlocks, and white feet are such markings. They are present at birth and do not change later; that is why they are entered as distinguishing features in the pony's papers. White spots that form as a result of pressure or injuries are not called markings.

Brands

In earlier times horses and ponies were marked with a brand to indicate ownership. In some countries this is still the practice. Where herds of horses are kept on huge pastures, brand marks help keep track when counting or vaccinating the horses and also offer protection against stealing. In some countries brands are used to indicate descent from certain ancestors. They are made by pressing an almost red-hot iron against the skin so briefly that the pony hardly feels it. (Foals are branded on the left haunch; the registry brand for stud book is on left side of the neck.)

How Ponies See, Hear, Smell, and Feel

The sense organs of ponies and horses have remained unchanged for millions of years and are designed for the way of life of a wild animal. This means that they are extremely sensitive to all external stimuli and impressions, especially to any signs of danger. When we handle a pony we must never forget that it does not see and hear the way we do. It sees everything both close by and at a distance with the same sharp clarity, and since its eyes are to the side of the head and somewhat slanted, its field of vision is wider than that of humans. Of course, it can only see forward and sideways. In order to see its surroundings in their entirety, it has to be able to move its head. If tight reins make this impossible, there is always the danger that the pony may get startled and shy (that is why pulling horses wear blinders). It is also worth knowing that horses have much better night vision than people.

58

Understanding Ponies

The sense of hearing is very highly developed in horses and ponies. The twitching ears pick up sounds by turning independently of each other in the direction from which a sound emanates. Wild horses have protected themselves from danger this way for eons. The sensitive ears of a horse perceive a much greater range of sounds than our ears do. Loud and sudden outbreaks of sound can therefore easily startle or frighten a pony, a fact that we should always remember. On the other hand, ponies are very receptive to soothing and pleasant sounds like humming and whistling and to music in general. Whenever I go by myself on a leisurely outing on my pony I always sing or whistle in time with the gait and enjoy watching the play of my pony's ears.

Apart from eyes and ears, ponies use their noses to perceive and explore their surroundings and also to keep away from danger. Their sense of smell is very acute. They sniff everything that is strange or not quite safe or that excites their curiosity. Everything that is worth examining is approached through the nostrils.

In ponies, as in humans, the sense of taste is closely linked to the sense of smell. It seems to me though, on the basis of my experience, that taste varies a lot among ponies. Animals that have grown up free in a pasture show no interest in sugar while stabled horses whose owners have introduced them to the bad habit of getting sugar as a treat beg for it. Ponies also differ in how easily they will take medicines. We had one pony that let us insert a certain kind of large capsule into its mouth without objecting. Our other horses swallowed this capsule happily, but this pony would check out the capsule by biting down on it, then pretend to swallow it while letting the unsavory liquid run out the side of its mouth.

The natural instinct to distinguish poisonous plants from edible ones is unfortunately no longer reliably present in ponies. That is why it is up to us to watch out for suspicious plants.

The sense of touch is especially important for ponies and horses. They "feel" their immediate surroundings through signals received by their feelerlike whiskers, their lips, and even the skin of their whole bodies. Especially sensitive parts of the body are the head, the neck, the withers and shoulders, the ribs, the flanks, and the lower legs. An alert pony will react instantly to the slightest flick of a whip on the shoulder or side. And we have all seen horses' and ponies' skin vibrate to drive off irritating flies. The pony's skin is just as receptive to touch that feels good. It registers pleasure when the pony rubs up against objects, rolls on the ground, or when other ponies nibble in places it cannot reach with its own teeth. The pony also enjoys a praising pat on the neck, a reassuring smack on the hindquarter, and above all petting, which it often invites by moving its head close to us. The sense of touch—and people are unfortunately not always aware of this—allows for the closest contact between us and our ponies. When the pony feels our soft, sensitive hands, our knees pressed close, and our relaxed thighs, a kind of contact is formed that can be called complete understanding.

Pony Nature

Character, Temperament, Feeling
Even though we can name some specific qualities—such as hardiness, resilience, stamina, trust, and charm—to give a general picture of the nature of ponies, there are other qualities that vary considerably from breed to

Understanding Ponies

breed. In addition—and anyone who has much to do with ponies can attest to this—each pony has its own individual nature that is made up of character, temperament, and feeling. This individuality, which lies deep inside, sometimes comes to the fore in an expression of the eyes, or we sense it in a gesture of loving affection or a reaction of displeasure. It is strongly affected by the experiences the pony has. Knowing this, we can see what a great responsibility we have toward the animal. We can improve the nature and talents of a pony, but we can also spoil it. The bad habits a pony may have like bucking, biting, and kicking are almost always acquired. A pony is born "wild" but not mean. The newborn foal is closer in nature to its distant ancestors than to the ways of its "well-trained" mother. Mistakes in handling made in its early life are practically impossible to remedy later.

Ponies often react very differently to different people. This is part of their psychological makeup; they remain highly sensitive in spite of their robustness. It is impossible to determine where a sympathy or antipathy originates, whether in the person, in the pony, or in something that happens between the two. But it is clear that ponies have a very sure "sense" of people and that this sense is incorruptible. There is no changing the pony's mind. The pony also senses all its master's feelings: fear or courage, hesitation or determination. All our moods can affect it.

The part of the pony's psyche that is least affected by external factors is its temperament. To be sure, unusually gloomy circumstances, such as being kept alone in a small, dark stall, will dampen its naturally lively spirit, and high-energy food can liven up a placid animal, but there will be no lasting change in the fundamental nature of the pony.

Instinct and Reflex, Intelligence and Learning Ability

The different kinds of behavior in a horse or pony can arise from instinct or be the result of mental activity, i.e., based on memory. Instinct and reflexes form the bridge between horses as we know them today and their distant ancestors. We must keep reminding ourselves that horses originally lived in wide-open spaces. This made them alert and curious but also shy and easily frightened. Horses have also always lived in herds. These original instincts and reflexes have been preserved through the thousands of years of association with human beings, and they are present in every newborn foal.

Ever since horses have been domesticated, man has made use of their ability to learn and has trained their intelligence. One often hears the foolish statement that horses are stupid. Anyone familiar with horses or ponies knows that this is nonsense; ponies, especially, can be very "clever." In our daily dealings with them we have constant proof of their excellent abilities to learn. They do not "think" or "reason" the same way we do, but they feel and observe, and they react to their feelings and observations. They are able to change their behavior on the basis of experience. What happens between the registering of an impression and the following reaction is often more complex than instinct or reflex, and we can quite rightly ascribe it to intelligence. The outstanding sense of orientation ponies have may be instinctive, but their amazing memory and their heightened attentiveness go beyond instinct. There are, of course, different degrees of intelligence. But if a particular horse or pony seems stupid, its faculties have probably been dulled by inappropriate treatment.

Understanding Ponies

Major Aspects of Behavior

A pony's behavior is the key to its nature. But this behavior is so complex and varied that I can refer here only to those aspects we need to be aware of to handle and care for ponies properly. Ignorance of basic patterns of behavior often causes problems, usually for the pony.

A pony yawns by drawing back the upper lip. Do not confuse this with the similar gesture of curling the lip.

A pony raises its head and curls the upper lip when it detects an interesting smell, especially during mating season or when it is curious about something.

Curling the Lip

I once saw a boy hit his pony on the upper lip because the animal was curling it up. He thought this was a bad habit like cribbing or windsucking (page 14) or weaving out of boredom. People often mistake a pony's curling the lip, during which the head is raised high and stretched forward with the upper lip pulled back, for yawning. But curling the lip is a natural reaction to unfamiliar or unpleasant smells and is an expression of curiosity and interest.

Rolling on the Ground

Rolling on the ground is another habit that is often misunderstood and punished. Granted, it is irritating when a pony that has been groomed to perfection before an outing makes for the only mud puddle in its pasture and rolls in it on returning home and being unsaddled. The pony does not do this deliberately to annoy its master but to express its delight at being loose again and to stimulate its skin. It is acting on a powerful instinct, and we should not try to restrain it but should rather provide a sandy paddock for the pony to roll in. Watch out if the pony rolls in its box; it might get stuck there.

Rolling on the ground is a sign that your pony is feeling especially happy and comfortable.

61

Understanding Ponies

Social Behavior

Watching several foals play in a pasture provides a good introduction to the behavior of ponies. We can observe approach and flight, friendship and squabbles. When grown ponies quarrel it is usually over food or to settle questions of rank. Showdowns over rank are normal occurrences in the context of social behavior, and we should not interfere unless a pony seems seriously threatened, which happens only rarely. If there is continual fighting over food, this is a different matter. Here we should solve the problem with separate feeding stations. If two ponies simply refuse to get along and express this by quarreling and serious biting, this too is a reason for us to step in and separate the antagonists.

"Pony Language"

The range of sounds ponies produce is large; it includes whinnying in all its variations, from squeaking, squealing, and screaming to snorting and a kind of snoring sound. Anyone who really knows and loves his pony can interpret its language. The position of the ears indicates the mood the pony is in. Pointed forward, they express curiosity, interest, and friendliness. If the ears are laid back flat, this can be a warning and a signal of aggressive behavior. But in my experience it often is no more than a sign of caution and timidity. The eyes too are a key to a pony's state of mind. They should be clear and alert. If they are half closed, the pony is dozing and totally relaxed. Be careful when you can see the whites of the eyes; this may signal a "fit of temper" or the contemplation of a mean act.

Multiple Gaits

Some breeds of horses and, among ponies, the Icelandic pony, have a special trait, namely, an inherent talent for several gaits. They may master not only the three basic gaits of walk, trot, and canter but are also able to do the running walk and thus be four-gaited. A pony with five gaits will also have pacing in its repertoire. The pace is a gait in which the horse or pony moves the lateral front and hind legs simultaneously. A good Icelandic pony with an expert rider can achieve gallop speeds at the pace. The running walk, which is defined by its name, is an ideal gait for covering great distances. It is easy on both pony and rider because of the minimal concussion involved and the fluidity of movement. But the smoothness of this gait does not mean that it is monotonous; the running walk should appear lively, accentuated, and energetic.

Riding and Driving a Pony

In the few pages of this chapter I will include only the most basic advice and tips for a young rider and driver of a pony, i.e., for the neophyte. I hope that my readers will be moved to consult specialized literature for additional crucial information (page 69).

Handling a Pony

The most important thing in dealing with a pony is mutual trust. If we approach a pony calmly, openly, and firmly, we will quickly gain its trust. Some basic rules are:
• Always approach a pony from the front, never from behind; walk around its head, not its tail end, so that it will not be startled and kick.
• Talk to the pony; your voice will put it at ease and make it feel secure.
• Never yell at your pony but always speak clearly and firmly to it.
• Never be violent, impatient, or hasty around your pony but always calm and relaxed.
• Do not make sudden movements or noises that might frighten the pony.
• Any rebuke (punishment) must follow immediately on the misbehavior (disobedience) for the connection between the two to be understood.
• Never hit to hurt! A loud swat with the flat of the hand serves perfectly well as a reprimand and will be understood by the pony as such.
• To express praise, pat the pony firmly on the neck or croup; timid stroking causes a tickling sensation for the pony.
• Offer treats (carrots, pieces of apple) on the flat of your hand.
• Never chase after your pony if it runs away; wait until it calms down and stops.
• Do not run away from a pony that is running toward you. Stand still and wave your arms; this will stop the pony.

The Appropriate Equipment

There is an almost overwhelming number of items on the market to satisfy every whim of today's horse or pony owner. How will you make the right choices from this confusing wealth of offerings? What should be your guiding principle? Whether you are buying riding clothes, a saddle, or saddle and bridle accessories, keep in mind that everything should reflect its intended use, that it should be of solid quality and workmanship, and that it has to fit. In rider's apparel these considerations have to be kept in mind, particularly for the breeches and boots. If the pants are too tight at the knee or the seat, they are unusable. Buy boots large enough so that they can be worn with wool socks in the winter. All leather equipment for the pony must be well made

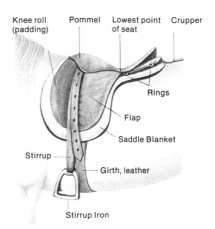

Knee roll (padding)   Pommel   Lowest point of seat   Crupper

Rings

Flap

Saddle Blanket

Stirrup

Girth, leather

Stirrup Iron

A pony saddle for pleasure riding and sport: flat saddle with panels, a deep seat, widely cut pommel, and straight, only slightly padded flaps. Saddle bags can be attached to the rings under the cantle. This kind of saddle should have a crupper for stability.

Riding and Driving a Pony

and of good fit. This is not the place to try to save money or to choose according to aesthetic principles. Cheap equipment can end up costing a great deal of money. Broken stirrup leathers or saddle girths are not cheap to replace.

What equipment do you really need? Someone who rides as a hobby needs nothing more to start than a pair of comfortable jeans, a shirt, blouse, or sweater, hard-soled shoes with heels, and a helmet secured by a harness. Even if you are starting riding lessons at a riding school or with a Pony Club you should confine yourself to essentials until you are sure you want to continue the riding program. Riding breeches and boots are expensive and children and young adults quickly grow out of them. In addition to these basic items, a complete outfit includes a riding jacket, a raincoat, riding gloves, and a whip. Spurs are used only rarely with ponies. For trail riding, boots that are not too high are best; and for bad weather a poncho that reaches down to the pony's croup is most useful. For small riders the main consideration is that the clothes be comfortable and that there be no possibility for the shoes to get entangled in the stirrup irons (avoid footwear with laces).

A riding pony's basic equipment consists of a bit and bridle, a complete saddle with saddle blanket, a halter, and a strap or rope for tying. The bit must not be too long or too narrow. It has to fit perfectly to insure good contact and to not injure the pony's sensitive mouth. The reins should provide a good grip; they may be made of plaited leather or of leather straps. Saddles come in all kinds of shapes and makes. There are dressage, jumping, and multipurpose saddles as well as special cross-country saddles that distribute the rider's weight along the full length of the pony's back. There are special saddles for some pony breeds, namely, for Fjord,

Haflinger, and Icelandic ponies. The panels on saddles for Icelandic ponies have lateral ridges to keep the saddle from slipping from side to side and are often equipped—like

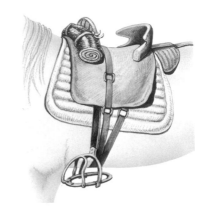

The cowboy saddle of the *gardians* in the Camargue; it is practical, comfortable, and secure. In a somewhat modified form it is used for trail riding. The basket stirrups provide the foot with a secure hold.

A Western saddle for ponies; this is both comfortable and secure, and especially well suited for trail riding.

64

Riding and Driving a Pony

many other pony saddles—with cruppers for better stability. Many trail riders favor Western saddles because they are comfortable and secure. These saddles are intended for a style of riding different from that common in the eastern United States and Europe, and they are unsuited for posting and jumping. Many young riders prefer a saddle pad, which for a pony is nothing more than a sheepskin or a blanket, to a regular saddle. But this is not recommended for fearful children or unconfident riders. Whatever saddle you choose, it has to sit perfectly on the pony's back and fit the rider. The quality and design of the stirrup irons is important too (especially for children). The stirrup irons should be heavy and wide so that a foot that has slipped out can find the iron easily and so that it does not get stuck in it in case of a fall. A rubber tread insures a good grip. Safety irons that release the foot in a fall are also recommended.

The tack for driving consists of harness, reins, and whip. Harnesses come in different styles depending on size and number of ponies, how they will be harnessed, and the kind of carriage to be pulled. Again the proper fit of the harness is crucial.

A Basic Riding Course

One cold winter day I saw a small boy gallop on his pony along an icy country road. The daring exploit ended happily in front of a small stable. When I asked the boy if he had learned how to ride, he answered with a laugh, "No, of course not, I know how to ride!" Such natural talents exist, particularly among children and young people. They mount a pony or horse for the first time and ride better than many of us do after many hours of classes. But these talents are rare. And since riding consists of more than just staying balanced on the horse's or pony's back—which is of course the crucial basic element—I would urge anyone to get a solid schooling in horsemanship, which includes not only practice but also theory. The safety of the rider is not the only thing to be concerned about in riding; we also have to think of the pony's safety and comfort. An untrained rider can also be a hazard in heavy traffic. If you want to drive ponies, training is mandatory. Controlling a pony and a buggy looks easier than it is. In contrast to the rider on horseback who can communicate directly with his pony through the reins and bit, his weight, and his legs, the driver's only aids are the reins and the whip. In addition, he can use the sounds produced by his voice and the crack of the whip.

Where should you go for horsemanship training? Nowadays there are riding schools or Pony Clubs in all areas of the country. The more than 300 local chapters of the United States Pony Clubs offer instruction in dressage, show jumping, combined training, and many other sports; and members receive certificates for proficiency at riding and teaching. For more advanced equestrian education, scores of colleges and universities around the country offer degrees in animal science and equine studies, and a variety of specialized schools offer certification as an instructor. The quality and cost of these programs vary widely, so a potential student should carefully investigate the options and talk to recent graduates. Also, since there is no nationwide licensing program for instructors or trainers in the United States, teaching certificates from American schools are of questionable value.

Riding and Driving a Pony

Learning to Ride

Several lessons without reins or saddle on a pony that is held by a longe rein are excellent for giving the novice rider a proper sense of the pony's movements and a secure seat. Longeing a pony means that the trainer stands in the middle of a ring, holding the pony by a longe rein about 24 feet (7 m) long and moving it around in a circle. To help in the initial stages of learning to ride, a wooden horse has been constructed on which the student can practice, repeatedly and at ease, things that might be torture for a horse. Unfortunately, this clever device is not found in many riding schools. For children, vaulting with ponies is a favorite preliminary exercise for horseback riding. They can start at seven to eight years. A class usually consists of eight children who, first singly, then in pairs or threes, do various gymnastic exercises on the pony galloping around the longeing circle.

A proper riding course should consist of at least one and preferably two hours a week. How long it will take to acquire the necessary basic skills will vary from person to person. You should never break off your training without good reason. For the recreational rider a certificate in basic horsemanship is a good thing to aim for. To get such a certificate the student has to demonstrate his or her knowledge and skills in a test that includes actual riding and theory. If you want to perfect your riding skills, there are advanced courses for competitive riding, dressage, jumping, and eventing.

The basic training for a pony driver includes all the skills necessary for driving with a single horse and with a team of two.

In the Countryside

There are many things to watch out for when we "go out" on horseback or with our horse and buggy. People on horseback and in horse-drawn vehicles have to obey all traffic laws. Drivers should check before every outing whether their carriage is in good working order (lights, brakes). If the carriage is left standing, the brakes have to be on, and the reins properly secured. The driver should know the traffic hand signals for turning and stopping.

For the horseback rider there is one paramount rule that always applies in town, in woods and fields, in bad weather, when resting, and when it gets dark, on short and long outings, or on long-distance rides. The rule is: caution on the road. Ride at a walk within town limits and keep to the far right-hand side of the road. If you ride in groups—never more than twenty-five riders—ride single file, one rider behind the other, with experienced equestrians at the head and tail. When you want to turn, give clear signals. If you ride in the countryside, stay on the available paths. Do not ride on bicycle and pedestrian paths. In the woods (never ride on closed roads), show consideration to the wild animals by being quiet. If you encounter other riders or people on foot, slow to a walk and say hello. Make sure you can be seen at dusk or night, in fog, or during heavy snowfall. Carry a lantern or flashlight on your left side or attach reflectors to your boots. If you ride in a group, the first rider carries a white lamp, the last rider a red one.

These rules may seem excessive or superfluous but they are based on experience that shows that riding can be dangerous. We should keep risk to a minimum. Still, every rider and driver should be covered by accident insurance and every pony owner should have liability insurance.

Riding and Driving a Pony

Sports

For most recreational riders riding is more than a hobby; it is part of what makes life worth living. An outing on horseback or in a sulky, carriage, or sled is the high point of the day. A long-distance ride during which we spend day and night, good weather and bad with our four-footed companion and experience amusing incidents and unpleasant surprises with him insures a complete break from the hectic tempo of our normal lives. All our restlessness vanishes when we wander through the countryside on our pony and hear it snorting and stamping near the campfire at night.

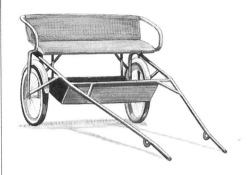

Pony cart for two

A pony carriage; four-seater with facing seats

In Europe the possibilities for pony-riding vacations are growing from year to year. Many countries offer "vacations in the saddle," among them Austria, Holland, Switzerland, Iceland, England, Ireland, and France, which is particularly famous for leisure riding. These vacations can be combined with other sports as well as with language courses. Riding courses are available for beginners as well as for advanced riders, and there are special courses in dressage, jumping, and eventing. Pony trekking is especially popular, and young riders or beginners are often allowed to participate. You should make detailed inquiries to prevent disappointment before you decide on a specific vacation. Recommendations and reports by friends can be a great help.

For many pony riders and drivers, performance and perfection in shows is what they are after. Playful contests are organized for young acrobats on horseback, and later there is a great variety of riding competitions that enthusiastic contestants can enter. The number of riders and drivers participating in events of all types shows how popular equestrian sports—and ponies—have become in recent years.

Pony Clubs

National Appaloosa Pony, Inc.
Eugene Hayden
PO Box 206
Gaston, IN 47342

American Connemara Pony Society
Mrs. John E. O'Brien
Hoshiekon Farm
RD 1
Goshen, CT 06756

International Icelandic Pony Association
Elizabeth Haug
Saga Ranch
3250 El Camino Real
Atascadero, CA 93422

American Miniature Horse Association
Dr. Leon B. Blair
611 Ryan Plaza Drive
Suite 1119
Arlington, TX 76011

Norwegian Fjord Horse Association
  of North America
Gene Bauer
29645 Callahan Road
Round Lake, IL 60073

Pony of the Americas Club
Phil Porter
PO Box 1447
Mason City, IA 50401

National Quarter Pony Association
Edward Ufferman
5135 County Road 25
Marengo, OH 43334

American Shetland Pony Club
Peggy Smith
PO Box 435
Folwer, IN 47944

American Walking Pony Registry
Mrs. Joan Hudson Brown
Rt. 5 Box 88
Upper River Road
Macon, GA 31211

American Welara Pony Society
Olivia Wiley
PO Box 401
Yucca Valley, CA 92284

Welsh Cob Society of America
Mrs. H. G. Ingersoll
400 Head of the Bay Road
Buzzards Bay, MA 02532

Welsh Pony Society of America
Mrs. Gail Headley Hamilton
PO Box 2977
Winchester, VA 22601

Index

Index

"Italic numbers" indicate color photos

Index

Perfect for Pet Owners!

PET OWNER'S MANUALS

Over 50 illustrations per book (20 or more color photos), 72–80 pp., paperback.

AFRICAN GRAY PARROTS (3773-1)
AMAZON PARROTS (4035-X)
BANTAMS (3687-5)
BEAGLES (9017-9)
BEEKEEPING (4089-9)
BOSTON TERRIERS (1696-3)
BOXERS (4036-8)
CANARIES (4611-0)
CATS (4442-8)
CHINCHILLAS (4037-6)
CHOW-CHOWS (3952-1)
CICHLIDS (4597-1)
COCKATIELS (4610-2)
COCKER SPANIELS (1478-2)
COCKATOOS (4159-3)
COLLIES (1875-3)
CONURES (4880-6)
DACHSHUNDS (1843-5)
DALMATIANS (4605-6)
DISCUS FISH (4669-2)
DOBERMAN PINSCHERS (9015-2)
DOGS (4822-9)
DOVES (1855-9)
DWARF RABBITS (1352-2)
ENGLISH SPRINGER SPANIELS (1778-1)
FEEDING AND SHELTERING BACKYARD
   BIRDS (4252-2)
FEEDING AND SHELTERING EUROPEAN
   BIRDS (2858-9)
FERRETS (9021-7)
GERBILS (9020-9)
GERMAN SHEPHERDS (2982-8)
GOLDEN RETRIEVERS (9019-5)
GOLDFISH (9016-0)
GOULDIAN FINCHES (4523-8)
GREAT DANES (1418-9)
GUINEA PIGS (4612-9)
GUPPIES, MOLLIES, AND PLATTIES (1497-9)
HAMSTERS (4439-8)
IRISH SETTERS (4663-3)
KEESHONDEN (1560-6)
KILLIFISH (4475-4)
LABRADOR RETRIEVERS (9018-7)
LHASA APSOS (3950-5)
LIZARDS IN THE TERRARIUM (3925-4)
LONGHAIRED CATS (2803-1)
LONG-TAILED PARAKEETS (1351-4)

LORIES AND LORIKEETS (1567-3)
LOVEBIRDS (9014-4)
MACAWS (4768-0)
MICE (2921-6)
MUTTS (4126-7)
MYNAHS (3688-3)
PARAKEETS (4437-1)
PARROTS (4823-7)
PERSIAN CATS (4405-3)
PIGEONS (4044-9)
POMERANIANS (4670-6)
PONIES (2856-2)
POODLES (2812-0)
POT BELLIES AND OTHER MINIATURE PIGS
   (1356-5)
PUGS (1824-9)
RABBITS (4440-1)
RATS (4535-1)
ROTTWEILERS (4483-5)
SCHNAUZERS (3949-1)
SCOTTISH FOLD CATS (4999-3)
SHAR-PEI (4334-2)
SHEEP (4091-0)
SHETLAND SHEEPDOGS (4264-6)
SHIH TZUS (4524-6)
SIAMESE CATS (4764-8)
SIBERIAN HUSKIES (4265-4)
SMALL DOGS (1951-2)
SNAKES (2813-9)
SPANIELS (2424-9)
TROPICAL FISH (4700-1)
TURTLES (4702-8)
WEST HIGHLAND WHITE TERRIERS (1950-4)
YORKSHIRE TERRIERS (4406-1)
ZEBRA FINCHES (3497-X)

NEW PET HANDBOOKS

Detailed, illustrated profiles (40–60 color photos), 144 pp., paperback.

NEW AQUARIUM FISH HANDBOOK (3682-4)
NEW AUSTRALIAN PARAKEET
   HANDBOOK (4739-7)
NEW BIRD HANDBOOK (4157-7)
NEW CANARY HANDBOOK (4879-2)
NEW CAT HANDBOOK (2922-4)
NEW COCKATIEL HANDBOOK (4201-8)
NEW DOG HANDBOOK (2857-0)
NEW DUCK HANDBOOK (4088-0)
NEW FINCH HANDBOOK (2859-7)
NEW GOAT HANDBOOK (4090-2)

NEW PARAKEET HANDBOOK (2985-2)
NEW PARROT HANDBOOK (3729-4)
NEW RABBIT HANDBOOK (4202-6)
NEW SALTWATER AQUARIUM
   HANDBOOK (4482-7)
NEW SOFTBILL HANDBOOK (4075-9)
NEW TERRIER HANDBOOK (3951-3)

REFERENCE BOOKS

Comprehensive, lavishly illustrated references (60–300 color photos), 136–176 pp., hardcover & paperback.

AQUARIUM FISH (1350-6)
AQUARIUM FISH BREEDING (4474-6)
AQUARIUM FISH SURVIVAL MANUAL
   (9391-7)
AQUARIUM PLANTS MANUAL (1687-4)
BEFORE YOU BUY THAT PUPPY (1750-1)
BEST PET NAME BOOK EVER, THE
   (4258-1)
CARING FOR YOUR SICK CAT (1726-9)
CAT CARE MANUAL (1767-6)
CIVILIZING YOUR PUPPY (4953-5)
COMMUNICATING WITH YOUR DOG
   (4203-4)
COMPLETE BOOK OF BUDGERIGARS
   (6059-8)
COMPLETE BOOK OF CAT CARE (4613-7)
COMPLETE BOOK OF DOG CARE (4158-5)
DOG CARE MANUAL (9163-9)
FEEDING YOUR PET BIRD (1521-3)
GOLDFISH AND ORNAMENTAL CARP
   (9286-4)
GUIDE TO A WELL BEHAVED CAT
   (1476-6)
GUIDE TO HOME PET GROOMING
   (4298-0)
HEALTHY CAT, HAPPY CAT (9136-1)
HEALTHY DOG, HAPPY DOG (1842-7)
HOP TO IT: A Guide to Training Your Pet
   Rabbit (4551-3)
HORSE CARE MANUAL (1133-3)
HOW TO TALK TO YOUR CAT (1749-8)
HOW TO TEACH YOUR OLD DOG
   NEW TRICKS (4544-0)
LABYRINTH FISH (5635-3)
MACAWS (9037-3)
NONVENOMOUS SNAKES (5632-9)
TROPICAL MARINE FISH
   SURVIVAL MANUAL (9372-0)

Barron's Educational Series, Inc. • 250 Wireless Blvd., Hauppauge, NY 11788
Call toll-free: 1-800-645-3476 • In Canada: Georgetown Book Warehouse
34 Armstrong Ave., Georgetown, Ont. L7G 4R9 • Call toll-free: 1-800-247-7160
ISBN prefix: 0-8120 • Order from your favorite book or pet store

(#62) R 7/95